Turner's Holland

FRED G.H. BACHRACH

Turner's Holland

TATE GALLERY

Exhibition sponsored by ABN AMRO Bank, Calor Gas and Makro

 ABN·AMRO Bank

front cover
**Van Tromp Returning after the
Battle off the Dogger Bank** 1833 (no.16)

frontispiece
Charles Martin **Sketch of J.M.W. Turner** 1844
Pencil on paper *National Portrait Gallery, London*

ISBN 1 85437 140 1

A catalogue record for this book is available from the British Library

Published by order of the Trustees 1994
for the exhibition of 26 July – 2 October 1994
Published by Tate Gallery Publications,
Millbank, London SW1P 4RG
© Tate Gallery 1994 All rights reserved
Designed by Caroline Johnston
Typeset in Baskerville by Tate Gallery Publications
and ICON Colour, London
Printed in Great Britain on 150gsm Parilux Cream
by Westerham Press, Edenbridge, Kent

Contents

Foreword

As is well known, Turner was an indefatigable traveller both at home and in continental Europe, but his various tours in the Netherlands have received little attention in print. For Professor Fred Bachrach, however, they have been a consuming enthusiasm for many years, and it brings us great pleasure to be able to publish and exhibit at least some of his copious researches into Turner in Holland.

Turner's Holland was not our Holland. For him it meant not the relatively small country of today, but the larger Kingdom of the United Netherlands including modern Belgium, incorporated under the Dutch House of Orange-Nassau by the Treaty of Paris in 1814 and only broken up in 1839. Thus it included the battlefield of Waterloo, scene of *the* epoch-making event of Turner's lifetime; his eagerness to see it occasioned his first tour of the Netherlands, in 1817. On this and subsequent visits he filled his sketchbooks with views of cities, canals, ships and the sea, and with his characteristic memoranda of the minutiae of life; they provided the raw materials for some of the most impressive of his exhibited pictures of Continental scenery.

As this exhibition shows, Holland – no less than Italy – was for Turner a land of art and of history. His career flourished at a time when the Dutch Old Masters were avidly collected in England, largely as a consequence of the sales of emigré collections in London after the French Revolution. The Prince Regent led the way with lavish purchases, and the Duke of Bridgewater spurred Turner's own interest – developed as a student at the Royal Academy Schools – by commissioning him to paint a companion to his recently acquired sea-piece by the great Dutch marine artist, Van de Velde.

Rembrandt and Cuyp – masters respectively of shadow and of golden light – were among Turner's favourite Old Masters, honoured and imitated in his own work, and he experimented also in the vibrant Dutch tradition of low-life, picaresque genre. When he painted scenes from or inspired by Dutch history – whether a moment in the domestic life of Rembrandt, or episodes from the Glorious Revolution of 1688 or from the career of a composite, semi-fictitious Admiral 'Van' Tromp – he cast them in an appropriate historicising style, based on Dutch painting of the same period.

Alas, we have been unable to borrow certain important paintings, but we have included them in this catalogue which we hope will serve as an essential book on its subject. Omissions may be lamented, but the inclusion of 'Calais Pier' should not surprise when we realise that it is among the earliest and grandest of Turner's essays in the tradition of Dutch marine painting; nor is the Cuypish 'Sun Rising through Vapour' misplaced, for Turner had thought of calling it 'Dutch Boats'. To the National Gallery, which has most generously contributed these splendid works, and to our other lenders, we extend our most sincere thanks.

We are especially grateful to Professor Bachrach for his devoted work on this exhibition, and for his perceptive catalogue. As a Dutchman, and a sailor with a lifetime's experience of Dutch waters, he has special insights to offer.

Our sponsors, ABN AMRO Bank, Calor Gas and Makro, have been generous in their support.

Nicholas Serota
Director

Sponsors' Forewords

ABN AMRO BANK

The works on display in *Turner's Holland* and those reproduced in this publication demonstrate the strong cultural links that have existed between Britain and the Netherlands over the centuries. Specifically, the works show the influence of Dutch art on one of Britain's finest artists.

ABN AMRO Bank is pleased that its co-sponsorship of this exhibition and partnership with the Tate Gallery will, through this international relationship, enable a wider audience to see the art inspired by Turner's Holland.

We at ABN AMRO Bank hope that you enjoy this exhibition of some of Turner's most beautiful works.

P.J. Kalff
Chairman, Managing Board, July 1994

CALOR GAS AND MAKRO

Calor Gas and Makro are delighted to co-sponsor *Turner's Holland*.

The exhibition provides Makro with the opportunity to continue its involvement in sponsorship of the arts. Calor Gas has for many years supported community projects and environmental initiatives.

It is therefore a great pleasure for both companies to work with the Tate Gallery for the first time and to enable visitors to see this superb exhibition.

Howard Robinson
Chief Executive,
Calor Group plc

Tony Steele
Managing Director,
Makro Self Service Wholesalers Limited

Acknowledgments

Turner has long proved an exceptionally powerful magnet for commentators and researchers, amateur and professional alike. It was in the context of the Anglo-Dutch exhibition of British Romantic landscape painters and their Dutch models, entitled *Schok der Herkenning/Shock of Recognition*, for the Mauritshuis at The Hague and the Tate Gallery in 1970–1, that I first succumbed. A major contributing factor in this was my love of sailing and the sea, but what really enthralled me was Turner's Dutch sketchbooks, which I was able to study in the British Museum's Department of Prints and Drawings where they were at that time still preserved. However, it was only after my academic duties at Leiden and Amsterdam came to an end upon attaining that ambiguous status of 'Emeritus', that I was in a position seriously to concentrate on the long-cherished wish of studying 'Turner's Holland'.

In the course of this immensely exciting enterprise much help and encouragement was received from friends, fellow Turnerites, and experts in various fields. I should like to use this opportunity to thank them all most warmly. To name but a few, my thanks go to Christopher Brown, J. Bruyn, Freek and Wif Frets, H.J.A. Dessens, Judy Egerton, John Gage, Luke Herrmann, Evelyn Joll, Michael Kitson, Peter van der Merwe, Cecilia Powell, Barry Price, Ken Rhodes, Michael Robinson, Margarita Russell, Rachel van der Wilden, and Andrew Wilton.

I owe a great debt of gratitude to the staff of the Tate Gallery and especially David Blayney Brown, Ann Chumbley, and the Tate Gallery Exhibitions and Publications departments for their patience and untiring assistance.

The National Gallery has been most generous. The Paul Mellon Center for Studies in British Art at New Haven, Connecticut, granted a month's Visiting Fellowship, which is greatly appreciated. But most of all I am indebted to my wife Harriet for unstinting editorial help and for support of an incurable sufferer of chronic Turneritis.

Fred G.H. Bachrach

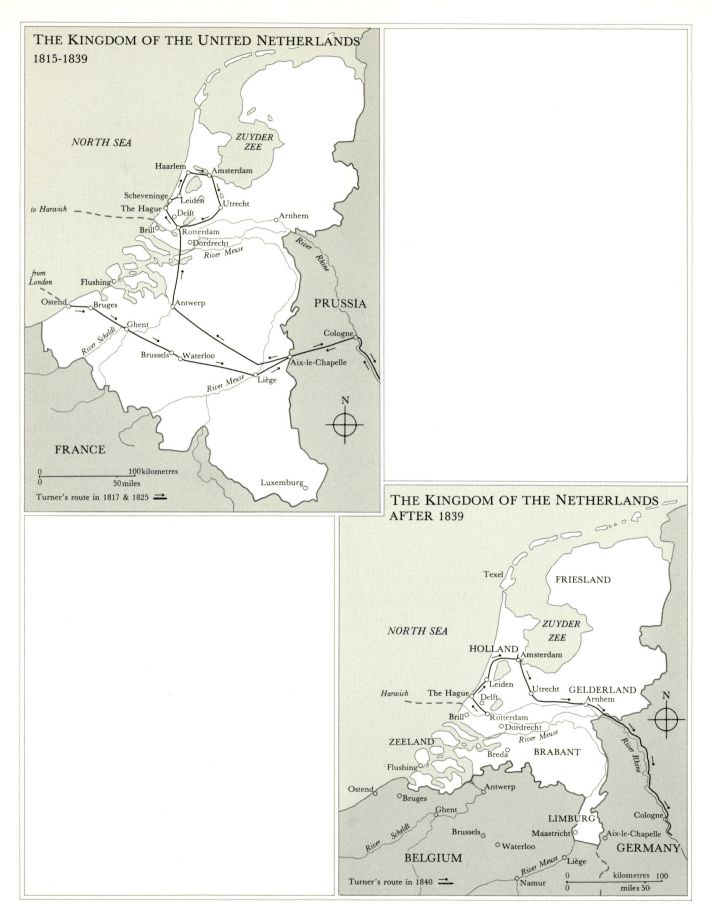

THE KINGDOM OF THE UNITED NETHERLANDS
1815-1839

NORTH SEA

ZUYDER ZEE

Haarlem
Amsterdam
Scheveninge
Leiden
The Hague
Delft
Utrecht
Arnhem
Brill
Rotterdam
Dordrecht
River Meuse
River Rhine

to Harwich

from London

Flushing
Ostend
Bruges
Antwerp
Ghent
Brussels
Waterloo
Liège
River Scheldt
River Meuse
Cologne
Aix-le-Chapelle

PRUSSIA

N

FRANCE

Luxemburg

0   100 kilometres
0   50 miles

Turner's route in 1817 & 1825 ⇉

THE KINGDOM OF THE NETHERLANDS
AFTER 1839

Texel
FRIESLAND

NORTH SEA

ZUYDER ZEE

HOLLAND
Amsterdam
Leiden
Utrecht
GELDERLAND
The Hague
Delft
Arnhem
Brill
Rotterdam
Dordrecht
River Meuse
River Rhine

Harwich

ZEELAND
Breda
BRABANT
Flushing
Ostend
Bruges
Antwerp
Ghent
LIMBURG
Maastricht
Cologne
Aix-le-Chapelle
Brussels
Waterloo
River Scheldt
GERMANY
BELGIUM
River Meuse
Liège
Namur

N

0   kilometres   100
0   miles 50

Turner's route in 1840 ⇉

Introduction

In 1781, Sir Joshua Reynolds, first President of the Royal Academy, wrote after his return from a tour of Holland:

> Painters should go to the Dutch School to learn the Art of painting, as they would go to a Grammar School to learn languages.[1]

As a student in 1790, J.M.W. Turner, who was to be Britain's greatest and most widely travelled landscape and marine painter, heard Sir Joshua's last *Discourse* and probably visited his studio. Later he travelled in the Low Countries himself. This was in 1817, 1825, 1840, 1841 and 1842 and on these tours of about a fortnight each he drew over six hundred impressions of Dutch sites and shipping scattered over eight sketchbooks, while in his London studio he painted at various times some twenty-four canvases with Dutch subjects or Dutch elements. Despite Reynolds's exhortation, however, what 'Holland' stood for in Turner's life and art has so far largely remained unexplored. It is true that Turner's Dutch-inspired works represent only a fraction of his immense overall production. But the significance of this fraction far outweighs its extent. The present exhibition intends to offer the viewer an idea of this long neglected significance.

For Turner there were two keys to Holland: one emotional and one physical. Curiously enough, the key that opened 'Holland' to him physically was the battlefield of Waterloo in present-day Belgium. But this happened many years after the world of Netherlandish culture had begun to open up for him emotionally. The latter came about through his regular confrontation from his earliest youth with the art of the Dutch Golden Age. During the years of his tuition, London received a steady stream of pictures, prints and drawings from the Continent, many of them Dutch. Whenever he had the opportunity Turner would admire these at exhibitions in the houses of senior colleagues or patrons, and when visiting picture dealers' rooms and special collections.

After such emotional unlocking of his mind to Dutch pictorial creativity while still in his teens, it was not until almost three decades later, when he was forty-two, that he was at last able to turn the physical key by making a visit to the Netherlands in person. This was not the Kingdom as we know it today but that of the newly created 'United Netherlands'. Following the first defeat and abdication of Napoleon in 1814 – which liberated Europe from French domination – Lord Castlereagh, the British Foreign Secretary, prevailed on the Allies and in particular on Prussia and Austria, to create a new, strong state at the mouths of the rivers Meuse, Rhine and Scheldt in order to help preserve the dearly bought balance of power. This new state became a monarchy under King William I, the former Prince William VI, son of Stadtholder William V of Orange-Nassau who, ever since the French had overrun and annexed his country in 1795, had been a refugee in London. The territory now consisted of the original Dutch Republic (the Northern Netherlands), together with Belgium (the Southern Netherlands), and the Grand-Duchy of Luxembourg.

But peace was not to last. Eleven months after being exiled to the Mediterranean island of Elba, Napoleon returned to France, reassembled an army, and restarted the war. It was his final defeat by the Allied forces under the Duke of Wellington at Waterloo on 18 June 1815 that definitively confirmed the new national frontiers of Continental Europe. As regards Holland (to use the name of the principal province by which the Netherlands was traditionally known), these new frontiers remained formally in place for twenty-five years, i.e. until 1839 when the Kingdom was reduced to its present size – a period which, but for the trip of 1840, covered Turner's main Dutch visits as well as a number of brief transits when on his way to Switzerland and Italy (see p.10).[2]

In Britain the year 1815 was a watershed, in both political and cultural terms. From July onwards, the Government invited plans for monuments to commemorate the victory of Waterloo, the press clamoured for a grand historical painting, and the British Institution organised a competition for the most worthy design with the far from negligible 'Premium' of £1,000.[3] But, like most of the verse and prose churned out for the occasion, the designs submitted to a specially constituted Committee of Taste proved replete with chauvinistic clichés and 'patronizing pictures ... with red coats, foolish faces, and labels of victory', as the radical newspaper, the *Examiner* sneered on 3 November 1816. Writers such as Byron, Coleridge, Southey, and Hazlitt were frankly disgusted with the entries – and so was Turner.[4]

As competitive as he was compassionate, Turner appears to have decided almost at once to produce a counterblast. But it was not before August of the following year, after he had finally discharged his obligations (which were particularly remunerative) to publishers of topographical engravings based on his watercolours, that he felt free to travel to Waterloo in order to gather documentation. The trip was undertaken in the wake of hundreds of the new type of British

fig.i Elisha Kirkall after Willem Van de Velde, 'Gust of Wind', mezzotint
National Maritime Museum, Greenwich

tourist who, lured to visit the battlefield by jingoistic posters (fig.vi on p.16), would, once on the Continent, frequently travel on to the now fashionably 'Romantic' Rhine.[5]

In 1817 both the port of Ostend, where Turner disembarked, and the village of Waterloo, which was his first target, were in the United Netherlands. This meant that when he landed in Ostend on Tuesday, 12 August 1817, Turner actually set foot on Dutch soil. From the scribbled timetable on the last page of his diminutive 'Itinerary Rhine Tour' sketchbook[6] we know that his tour began with a quick passage through the Flemish towns of Bruges and Ghent as far as Brussels, followed by a full day absorbing impressions of the field of Waterloo. He then continued east, via the main Walloon cities, to Aix-la-Chapelle and Cologne. From there he travelled up the Middle Rhine as far as Mainz. Finally, after going downstream again as far as Cologne and this time crossing Flanders from east to west, he was in a position to enter Holland proper via Antwerp: by Thursday, 4 September, he could start exploring the physical world of the Dutch Masters.

If imported Dutch art of the seventeenth century was the emotional key to Turner's 'Holland', this should be qualified

as applying above all to Dutch marine art. Supporting evidence for this is provided by one of Turner's first biographers, who recorded that years later Turner found himself unexpectedly facing 'a green mezzotinto – an upright' after the Dutch marine-artist Willem Van de Velde, and said, with obvious emotion 'Ah! That made me a painter.'[7] It represented 'a single large vessel running before the wind and bearing up bravely against the waves' (fig.i). The story is plausible. As a boy Turner was fascinated by the sea-going vessels moored in the Pool of London (not far from his father's barbershop in Covent Garden), and he would often stay with a maternal uncle at Margate. There he clearly developed a special attachment to fishing-folk and a profound, no doubt basically 'escapist', love of the sea. Indeed, Turner's first exhibited oil painting was a marine, 'Fishermen at Sea' 1796 (Tate Gallery; B&J 1) and the picture with which he first made his name was 'Dutch Boats in a Gale; Fishermen Endeavouring to Put their Fish on Board' exh.1801 (no.1). Could anything be more symbolic, one feels, than these two 'firsts'?

'Dutch Boats in a Gale' was commissioned by the third Duke of Bridgewater, the Dutch-inspired canal builder known as the 'Father of British Inland Waterways',[8] who had also acquired a new interest in picture collecting. It was to be a companion piece to another Van de Velde marine, 'A Rising Gale', which this novice art-lover had recently purchased (fig.1b on p.29). The result, when shown at the Royal Academy exhibition, was a resounding success. However, although evidently 'seventeenth-century Dutch' in conception, it was dominated by a typically eighteenth-century English 'Sublimity' effect, as shown by the near-catastrophe of the carefully composed collision course of the two principal boats (fig.1a on p.28). This dramatic motif had clearly been derived from the widely read *Philosophical Enquiry into the Origin of our Ideas of the Sublime and the Beautiful* (1757) in which Edmund Burke postulated for 'Sublimity' the dark, the vast, the rough, and the danger-filled, but for the 'Beautiful' the smooth, the varied, and the peace-suffused, both in art and literature. The composition had been arrived at after a number of highly revealing preliminary studies in a former Academy sketchbook with blue-tinted paper (figs.1c–f on p.29), and the final result became the equivalent of a modern 'Picture of the Year'. Within a mere twelve months, its artist had been elected to full Membership of the Royal Academy of Art – a distinction which, at twenty-seven, made him the youngest RA in its entire history.

In the field of art history, and in contrast to what may be termed 'idealising and classicising' Italian art – 'realistic' Dutch art (and not only Dutch marine art) played an increasingly important role for British connoisseurs and artists during the eighteenth and nineteenth centuries. The Van de Veldes, father and son, had settled in England in 1672 and had been appointed Marine Painters to Charles II. Dutch Masters such as Aelbert Cuyp, Jacob van Ruisdael, Meindert

Hobbema, or Jan van Goyen, David Teniers (who was Flemish) and, above all, Rembrandt, were represented in many collections and at practically every auction.[9] Some British artists, moreover, such as Thomas Gainsborough, John Constable or John Crome, regularly modelled themselves on the Dutch landscape painters.[10]

For the less affluent, in an age before public galleries and museums, knowledge of many artists' work was spread not by their pictures but by prints. Through engraving, by then almost a cultural mass-medium, Rembrandt had become quite the rage in eighteenth-century Britain – if not yet an industry for forgers. There was 'a Madness to have his Prints', wrote a letter-writer to the press when warning against fakes.[11] Turner himself was not immune to the strong pull of 'Rembrandtism'.

As a conscientious ex-pupil of the Royal Academy Schools, he assiduously heeded the former President's admonition to go to the Dutch School 'as to a Grammar School'. Although he had started his career as a watercolour draughtsman, 'Fishermen at Sea' was a striking night-piece that, no matter how much influenced by British painters like Philip De Loutherbourg and Joseph Wright of Derby or the Dutch Master Aert van der Neer, eloquently demonstrated his interest in Rembrandt's use of two different sources of light. In his painting Turner skilfully employed the same technique, with light coming from both the moon over the Needles of the Isle of Wight and the red lantern in the boat's stern. In 1801 Benjamin West, the successor to Reynolds as President of the Royal Academy, commented on Turner's 'Dutch Boats in a Gale' with the extraordinary remark 'what Rembrandt thought of, but could not do', while Henry Fuseli, the Academy's Professor of Painting, had called it 'quite Rembrandtish'. Both reactions were typical of the taste of the time.[12]

After 'Dutch Boats in a Gale', the year 1802 provided the next manifestation of Turner's 'Dutch connection'. Like many of his countrymen during the short-lived Peace of Amiens with France, in that year Turner was able to visit the Continent for the first time. His goal was the Swiss Alps in order to make a number of drawings, but from the point of view of Turner's development as a painter, hardly less significant a result of the tour came from his visit to Paris on the return journey. For it was in Paris – of which, oddly enough, no topographical sketches seem to be extant – that he took the opportunity to study the incredibly rich hoard of works of art looted by Napoleon on his European conquests and newly exhibited at the Louvre. In his 'Studies in the Louvre' notebook (TB LXXII) Turner made sketches of some two dozen pictures that had particularly impressed him, adding on separate pages critical comments and detailed analyses. Among this selection there were three Rembrandts and two Ruisdaels.[13] But for many years thereafter, Turner's experience of the Louvre's Dutch Masters remained, as it were, 'on hold'.

In 1802, back in London, he again picked up the sketchbook that had served him for his studies for 'Dutch Boats in a Gale'. In it he drew no less than five views of the nerve-racking ordeal which occurred on the outward journey, when the ferry on which he was travelling was obliged to wait for high tide outside Calais bar. Together with a number of other passengers, equally impatient after their long war-time isolation, he had insisted on being rowed ashore in the ship's boat. In this operation they were nearly swamped on landing, as he noted in the margin of one of these sketches (fig.2b on p.31).

Subsequently, Turner called the sketchbook his 'Calais Pier' sketchbook (TB LXXXI), since in it he had drawn the most important studies on which not only his famous oil painting, 'Calais Pier, with French Poissards Preparing for Sea; An English Packet Arriving' exh.1803 (no.2) but also the smaller 'Fishing Boats Entering Calais Harbour' c.1803 (no.3) were based: a mezzotint of the latter, prepared by Turner himself, was included in his manual of landscape styles, the *Liber Studiorum* (fig.3a on p.32).[14]

Of course, the first point to stress about the two Calais pictures is the fact that the port of Calais is not situated on the Dutch coast! The reason for the inclusion of 'Calais Pier' in this catalogue is first, that for generations Calais had been the entry-port for visitors to the Netherlands who wanted to spend the shortest time at sea; secondly, the picture again demonstrates, in several important details, Turner's markedly personal response to the Dutch marine tradition. Moreover, 'Calais Pier' shows a thematic link with 'Dutch Boats in a Gale' (no.1) through the threatened collision between the central fishing-vessel – whose skipper, by lowering her gaff, is spilling the wind from her mainsail in order to take avoiding action – and the close-hauled incoming ferryboat whose passengers and crew are massed to leeward, anxiously watching the progress of events (fig.ii on p.14).

But there is more. To the 'Sublimity' of the scene – the potential catastrophe – Turner added in the right foreground its very opposite: the foolish group in their small boat, frantically trying with only one oar (and a bottle of, undoubtedly, 'Dutch' courage, proffered by a scolding fishwife) to avoid being flung against the pier while 'preparing for sea' (fig.iii on p.14). Quite apart from their obvious compositional function, the artist's intention here was surely to show that 'from the Sublime to the Ridiculous' (as he had copied out in a note in an earlier sketchbook) there was 'only a small step'.[15]

Up to a point, the same may be said of 'Fishing-Boats Entering Calais Harbour' (no.3), in which the danger of the central vessels' course must have been perfectly clear to informed nineteenth-century viewers; to such viewers, the boy's hopeless attempt to adjust a halyard while clinging to the mast and sprit of the nearest boat would have been recognised at once as 'Ridiculous' – a pictorial 'rider' to the painting's narrative content (which Turner later eliminated in his mezzotint). In both pictures, the ambiguity of British feelings about the French must not be overlooked, either – nor the

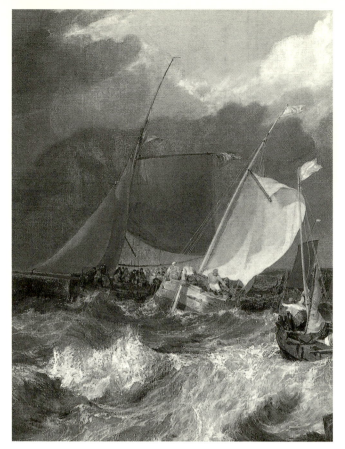

fig.ii Detail from 'Calais Pier, with French Poissards Preparing for Sea; an English Packet Arriving' exh.1803 (no.2)

fig.iii Detail from 'Calais Pier, with French Poissards Preparing for Sea; an English Packet Arriving' exh.1803 (no.2)

implied problems of the British when approaching 'Europe'.

Turner's real achievement in his Dutch-inspired marines was in depicting the wind. Indeed, as he remarked in one of his lectures, some eight years later, as Professor of Perspective at the Royal Academy, one word was sufficient to establish what is 'the greatest difficulty of the painter's art: to produce wavy air, as some call *the wind* ... To give that wind ... he must give the cause as well as the effect ... with mechanical hints of the strength of nature perpetually trammelled with mechanical shackles.'[16] Sailing is, after all, the harnessing of the wind 'with mechanical shackles'. And do not Turner's near-collisions at sea magnificently reveal his mastery of that 'greatest difficulty of the painter's art'? This was the natural complement to one of his most enduring characteristics, namely his interest in what John Gage has termed 'narrative expressed through weather'.[17]

Throughout his career Turner was passionately interested in what went on around him and in what, to him, was important in the past of the countries whose art he admired. This interest accounts for extraordinary references to Dutch history among his subjects. He was a voracious, albeit haphazard, reader – which enabled him, whenever he felt strongly about a political issue in Britain, to depict a historical parallel as a kind of allegory – an allegory in which Coleridge's famous distinction between 'fancy' and 'imagination' allowed each to play their part. In fact, his next 'Dutch' picture happens to be the first in which a reference to Dutch – specifically, Dutch maritime – history was employed to offer a contemporary political message to Britain. This was in 'Boats Carrying out Anchors and Cables to Dutch Men of War' c.1804 (no.4), a picture that clearly implied a warning to the Government to avoid repeating the complacency shown after the English victory against the Dutch off Lowestoft in 1665. Two years later, towards the end of the Second Dutch War, the spectacular raid up the Medway by a Dutch fleet that had refitted much faster than expected, had taken the authorities utterly by surprise. Now, in 1804, the artist appears to suggest that even after Nelson's victories, a French invasion might likewise still be launched at any time![18] In 1804, the threat of invasion from a French army massed in the Pas de Calais was at its height, despite earlier British victories at sea, and Turner's picture could therefore be said to have a highly topical reference. But the daily press failed to see the point. One newspaper even mocked in landlubberly innocence that Turner's sea seemed to have been painted 'with *birchbroom* and *whitening*' and that his historical reference was uncalled for.[19]

Three years later, in 1807, Turner exhibited 'Sun Rising through Vapour; Fishermen Cleaning and Selling Fish' (no.5). Also described by him as 'Dutch Boats' and as 'Dutch Boats and Fish-Market',[20] this picture has indeed strong Dutch echoes. Yet in several respects it is also utterly un-Dutch. Holland's North-Sea coast faces West, i.e. where the sun sets, and so the locality depicted for a 'sun rising' from open sea could not really be a beach on the mainland. Nor is the tidal height, as indicated by the pierhead, ever reached anywhere in the Netherlands except at a few points in the island province of Zeeland. The pier in the picture is, in fact, reminiscent of Turner's earlier 'Old Margate Pier' 1804 (private collection; B&J 51).

However, as already obvious in preliminary studies, there are unmistakably Dutch elements in the composition. In the finished picture, the boats on the left recall Van de Capelle, the man-of-war in the centre is pure Van de Velde, and the group of figures on the right (in seventeenth-century costume and evidently an afterthought) is Teniers all over – although no Dutch fishing folk would ever swill drinks from wine-glasses while 'cleaning and selling fish' on a beach at dawn. However, if (as Constable was to maintain[21]) it is the sky that is the keynote of any landscape, this was never more so than in this picture's brilliant emulation of both Cuyp and Claude.

The painting was not unanimously praised. Nonetheless, Turner set such high store by it that, after selling it to Sir John Leicester – for whose benefit, it may be recalled, he had referred to it as 'Dutch Boats' – he later bought it back at the auction of his late patron's collection in 1827. In his will of 1831, he even stipulated that it should hang between two pictures by Claude in the National Gallery when after his own death his oeuvre would go to the nation.

After 'Sun Rising through Vapour', Turner painted several 'ironically-intended' Anglo-Dutch genre-pieces with Rembrandtesque overtones, such as 'A Country-Blacksmith' 1807 (Tate Gallery; B&J 68), 'The Unpaid Bill' exh.1808 (no.6) and 'The Garreteer's Petition' 1809 (Tate Gallery; B&J 100), as well as Dutch-influenced landscapes such as 'Tabley' 1809 (Petworth; B&J 99) and 'Grand Junction Canal' 1810 (private collection; B&J 101), or his series of 'Cuypish' Thames pastorals. The first three canvases show Turner happily appropriating a major development in contemporary painting, the picturesque everyday-life scene.[22] And all of them bear testimony to the fact that his Dutch interest was not limited to marines or 'drolleries'. Inevitably, his pictorial models continued to be such Old Master pictures as regularly appeared in London sale-rooms and collections; while the Napoleonic wars still prevented travellers from actually landing in the Netherlands for almost another decade, these wars did, after all, cause the English art-market to boom.

One further point: 'The Garreteer's Petition' is more than an exercise in Dutch-inspired genre, humorously linked to 'The Distressed Poet' by Hogarth (Birmingham City Art Gallery). In the Royal Academy catalogue Turner appended for the first time verses of his own, ending with an entreaty to his Muse to 'finish well my long, my *long-sought* line'; as well as being a painter, Turner was a versifier, and would have known – and wanted his audience to know – the agony of creative expression, even if an element of self-irony cannot be denied.[23]

fig.iv 'Itinerary Rhine Tour' sketchbook 1817 (TB CLIX 101)

When at long last, in 1817, the time came for his first visit to Holland, Turner made brief notes in his 'Itinerary Rhine Tour' sketchbook (TB CLIX) planning what to see, where to stay, distances and prices.[24] A few of these jottings, as a note about the loss of his copy of the little vademecum reveals (fig.iv),[25] are taken from Charles Campbell's *The Traveller's Complete Guide through Belgium and Holland*, first published in 1815 and revised in 1817, but most of the data and keywords dealing with the Low Countries were taken from *Sketches in Flanders and Holland*, published in 1816 by his fellow-artist Robert Hills[26] (fig.v); Turner's very first page, superscribed 'Ostend', and whole passages copied verbatim, such as a list of useful Dutch phrases with their amateurish phonetic transcriptions, establish this debt.[27]

Turner's incredibly rapid pictorial notes on this tour, sometimes six to a page, all speak for themselves. They vividly reveal what arrested his attention – and what he apparently at once thought he might use for future painting; many leaves even contain miniature compositions for complete pictures.[28] His first destination, though, was the battlefield of Waterloo.

In the 'Waterloo and Rhine' sketchbook (TB CLX), after a number of pencilled impressions of peaceful Flemish towns between the coast and Brussels, a series of seventeen leaves shows the depth of emotion with which on Saturday, 16

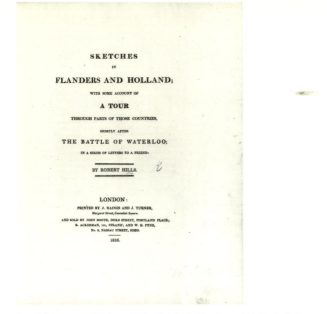

fig.v Title-page of Robert Hills, *Sketches in Flanders and Holland*, 1816

fig.vi Poster of 'Field of Waterloo', distributed to English-speaking travellers aiming for the battlefield, with an extract from Bradshaw's *Contintental Guide*

August 1817, Turner wandered across the historic battlefield. It was utterly bleak and empty, which made it all the more poignant an experience for one who, at every step he took, must have been conscious of the slaughter and suffering that had taken place there.

When in 1815 Hills passed through Ostend, this was only a few weeks after the battle. At that time, he still encountered long columns of British troops with their equipment and their wounded, wearily making their way to embarkation. Published the next year, his title-page specifically told the prospective reader (in capital letters) that it had been written 'shortly after The Battle of Waterloo'. The second edition of Campbell's *Guide* included an extra chapter, entitled 'A Walk over the Field of Battle at Waterloo' with quotations from poems by Sir Walter Scott and Robert Southey. Detailed descriptions of the battle itself 'By a Near Observer', provided with illustrations and maps, were reprinted time and time again.

Turner could thus fall back on a good deal of preliminary information at second hand. However, actually being on the spot himself and guided by locals who would eagerly point out where Sir Thomas Picton fell and where the young Prince of Orange was wounded, proved so much more harrowing than anything he had read, that he could not help scribbling across some of his sketches touching details such as '4000 killed here', '1500 killed here' or 'hollow where the great carnage took place of the Cuirassiers by the Guards'. The latter inscription occurs on a sketch (with superimposed plans) of the gate and ruins of the manor-house of Hougoumont (fig.7f on p.39). It was the heroic holding of this fortified farm by the Scots and Coldstream Guards against all French onslaughts that was the feat on which, in the words of the Duke of Wellington himself, the outcome of the battle had hinged. Counting the cost afterwards, the Allied Commander-in-Chief had confessed: 'Next to a battle lost, the worst is a battle won.' And so it became this location that the artist chose to paint.

In 'The Field of Waterloo' exh.1818 (no.7), Turner's supreme anti-war picture, the only living figures are women.[29] In despair they search by torchlight for their nearest and dearest in the mound of dead horses and soldiers, both Allied and French, in front of the burning manor-house. A flare has been fired by the last remaining troops to frighten off marauders. In the palette Turner chose for this completely unprecedented 'Guards-picture' in a war context, there is a violent clash between light and dark, comparable to that in Rembrandt's 'Guards-picture' in a peace context, the 'Night Watch' (Rijksmuseum, Amsterdam), which was specially noted in the 'Itinerary Rhine Tour' sketchbook as 'Corps de Guarde' and not to be missed in Amsterdam.[30] In the uniforms and saddle-cloths of the slain, through the ciphers 'G III' and 'N', particularly clear in his preliminary watercolour (without women), the tragic union in death of irreconcilably

INTRODUCTION

fig.vii Albert Cuyp, 'The Maas at Dordrecht' c.1660, oil on canvas
Andrew W. Mellon Collection. National Gallery of Art, Washington

conflicting political allegiances in life is poignantly emphasised (no.8). It is exactly what Byron expressed in his lines from Canto III of *Childe Harold's Pilgrimage* about 'rider and horse – friend, foe – in one red burial blent' – lines which, prior to quoting them in his catalogue entry,[31] Turner would have read in the *Times* of 3 November 1816:

Last noon beheld them full of lusty life
Last eve in Beauty's circle proudly gay,
The midnight brought the signal-sound of strife,
The morn the marshalling in arms – the day
Battle's magnificently stern array!
The thunder-clouds close o'er it, which when rent
The earth is cover'd thick with other clay,
Which her own clay shall cover, heap'd and pent,
Rider and horse – friend, foe – in one red burial blent!

The painting was a flop with the general public. In the continued national euphoria about 'their' victory, the almost total rejection of Turner's elegiac commemoration of 'Waterloo' seems typical. It was the very opposite of what the British Institution had expected in 1816 and, in spite of Hazlitt's sensitive appreciation in the *Examiner*,[32] one reviewer even likened the scene to 'a drunken hubbub on an illumination night'.[33] And so the picture returned to Turner and remained unexhibited for another 162 years until 1980 – which did not prevent him producing watercolours such as the one already mentioned of the gate of Hougoumont, and one of the road at the farm of La Haye Sainte, commissioned

for later engravings illustrating editions of the complete works of Byron and Scott (figs.8a–b on p.41).

The other Dutch-inspired picture that Turner showed in the Royal Academy's 1818 exhibition was 'Dort, or Dordrecht. The Dort Packet-Boat from Rotterdam Becalmed' (no.9) and a greater contrast is hardly imaginable. Yet both are connected by more than merely the year in which they were painted. For, if 'The Field of Waterloo' was intensely 'Sublime', the 'Dort' was a perfect embodiment of the 'Beautiful' – in the Burkean sense, that is. The brilliant September sky and the glassy water on which the practically immobilised packet-boat drifts, with her sails almost slack and her passengers and crew eagerly stocking up on fresh food from the farmers' wives in the chandlers' dinghies that customarily came alongside on this particular stretch of the river, all this makes the 'Dort' a perfect counterpoint to the 'Field of Waterloo' (no.7). It would seem that to Turner, after the tremendous psychological effort of rendering the essence of his Waterloo experience, the happy memory of the sunny, life-enhancing hours before the peaceful city of Dordrecht with its celebrated church tower and numerous boats dreaming at their moorings, just cried out to be painted.

The city of Dort (the local abbreviation for Dordrecht) would have been particularly intriguing to him because it was the birthplace of Aelbert Cuyp (1620–1691), many of whose pictures he must have seen in England. He admired him not only to the extent of modelling his Dort packet-boat on Cuyp's 'The Maas at Dordrecht' (fig.vii) and 'The Embarka-

[17]

fig.viii Augustus Wall Callcott, 'Entrance to the Pool of London' exh.1816, oil on canvas *With the consent of the Trustees of the Bowood Collection*

tion of Prince Frederick Henry' (Duke of Sutherland Collection), but also by scribbling underneath some sketches of the town's environs with ruminating cows and the urban horizon in the distance, the single word 'Cyp' (according to the English pronunciation) or – as on his next visit – 'quite a Cyp', whenever the view reminded him forcefully of the Master.

It has been argued that Turner's rival, Augustus Wall Callcott had provided, with his popular picture of the 'Entrance to the Pool of London' 1816 (fig.viii), a special stimulus to the 'Dort'.[34] There are indeed certain similarities. But we have a small compositional sketch of the 'Dort', after a set of sundry studies of military uniforms (and two of mourning women) in another of Turner's little notebooks, the 'Guards' sketchbook, which can only date from after his return from Holland.[35] The combination within the same notebook of material used for both paintings indicates that Turner may have been thinking in terms of a contrasting pair from very early on when starting work on 'The Field of Waterloo', irrespective of Callcott – even if, at some time or other, he also drew on a page in the 'Itinerary Rhine Tour' sketchbook a similar composition to the one in the 'Guards' sketchbook (fig.9b on p.43). Besides, for the final picture, he could draw on half a dozen sketches in the 'Dort' sketchbook,[36] including an extensive record of parts of the packet-boat herself, accurate down to the sculptured swan on her helm, echoing her name.

The 'Dort' was hailed as a major achievement by the press and in retrospect proves to have heralded the artist's new, lighter palette, usually associated with his first Italian tour of

the year after. Turner produced these two outstanding pictures as the only immediate fruits on canvas of his first Dutch tour. His 'Dort' sketchbook, however, includes dozens of delightful pencil sketches made on this trip, mostly of Dordrecht and Rotterdam, but also some of The Hague, Scheveningen, Haarlem, Amsterdam, Utrecht and a few other Dutch places; he constantly drew what he saw – and only really saw what he drew, successive views showing that each time his field of vision was almost semi-circular.

In 1819 Turner painted a third picture based on his Dutch tour. This was 'Entrance of the Meuse. Orange-Merchant on the Bar Going to Pieces; Brill Bearing S.E., Masensluys E. by S.' (no.10). Once again the composition offers a combination of the 'Sublime' and the 'Ridiculous', the former being produced by the wreck of the stranded merchant-vessel, the latter by the comic figures in small boats, prominently depicted in their eager groping for the little that was washed overboard of the Orangeman's juicy cargo.

With its explicit localisation of the catastrophe given by the bearings on the towns of Brill and Masensluys, whose meticulously painted profiles form the background, the artist suggests in his pun on the House of Orange that the picture is far more than the illustration of a familiar event – even though the *Times* of 16 January 1819 had reported the wrecking off Whitehaven of a schooner with oranges. As a matter of fact, the House of Orange was in some financial trouble. During the Stadtholderships of William V (died 1806) and of his son, William VI (who spent the years 1793–1813 in exile in

Britain), the family had made huge investments on the London stockmarket, and subsequently incurred heavy losses through the decline in the value of the pound after the Bank of England started selling off its bullion and forcing the acceptance of notes or silver for gold in 1817/18. As a result, while the dynasty was not exactly 'going to pieces' financially, such developments did not bode well to friends of Holland. And Turner could certainly be counted as one of these friends, if only as an observer of the disaster from a distance – like the wreck in the background of his picture.

It was to be another six years before the by now fifty year old artist visited Holland a second time. On 27 August 1825 he dined at the London house of his old friend and patron Walter Fawkes, who had bought the 'Dort' at its first showing in 1818 (the picture was hung in the music-room at Farnley Hall, of which the painter had made a delightful watercolour; fig.ix). Fawkes was now terminally ill. But Turner had to tell him (Mrs Fawkes noted in her *Diary*) that the next morning he was going to The Hague.[37]

As in 1817, it is only his extant sketches – in the 'Holland' and the 'Holland, Meuse and Cologne' sketchbooks[38] – which, despite their random order, allow us approximately to trace Turner's route from the views recorded. He travelled from Dover to Rotterdam, via Hellevoetsluis, then via Delft to The Hague, Leiden, Haarlem and Amsterdam, and next via Utrecht and Maastricht to Cologne. From there he went to Aix-la-Chapelle, Liège, Antwerp, Ghent and Bruges to Ostend, returning again via Dover. As is also apparent from his sketchbooks of other European travels, he consistently revisited the same places, again and again sketching in varying styles the same views or buildings, as if to check previous impressions and test his memory for detail.

This time he did not look for fisher folk, as he had done in 1817 when he made a whole series of sketches on Scheveningen beach, inspired no doubt by memories of Van de Velde or De Vlieger,[39] but concentrated on the towers and canals of Rotterdam and Amsterdam, reminiscent of pictures or engravings by Ruisdael, Rembrandt and Van der Heyden. One flimsy sketch has 'Hobbema' in the margin. Then there are copies of pictures in the Amsterdam museum, such as one of Gerard Terborch's 'The Parental Visit', with a special inscription for the young lady's 'beautiful satin' – an effect already remarked upon by Reynolds forty-four years earlier[40] (without either viewer presumably noting the scene's lewd ambiguity). Curiously enough, Turner did not draw any church interiors or views from aloft, but simple people going about their business, costumes, markets, town profiles, buildings, and ships.

In 1827 he exhibited two unusual 'Dutch' pictures at the Academy: 'Rembrandt's Daughter' (no.12) and 'Port Ruysdael' (no.11). The former was a pastiche of a Rembrandt then belonging to his colleague Sir Thomas Lawrence, 'Joseph and Potiphar's Wife' (fig.12a on p.48) and shows a renewed

fig.ix 'The Music Room, Farnley Hall' 1818, bodycolour on buff paper
Private Collection

interest in the Rembrandtesque which would lead to 'Pilate Washing his Hands' 1830 (no.13) and 'Jessica' 1830 (Petworth; B&J 333).

'Port Ruysdael' was another form of homage to a much-admired Dutch Master, whose works in the Louvre had provoked Turner to some very personal, if youthful criticism, as long ago as 1802. In the case of Rembrandt he had commented on the Master's 'Good Samaritan', on 'The Angel Departeth from Tobit Family', and on 'Susanna'; the Ruisdaels examined in Paris were 'The Burst of Sunlight' and 'A Storm on the Dikes of Holland'.

At the time, Turner noted in his 'Studies in the Louvre' sketchbook underneath 'Landscape by G Rysdael [*sic*]': 'a fine coloured grey picture, full of truth, and fin[e]ly treated as to light which falls on the middle ground, all beyond is of a true deep ton'd greyish green.' After this he became critical, continuing 'the Sky rather heavy but well managed but possesses too much of the Picture and the light. the Objects near to the light are poor and ill-jud[g]ed'.[41]

His comment on the picture underneath 'Sea [gap] Port [gap] Rysdael', starts with: 'a Brown picture, which pervades thro' the waters so as to check the idea of it being liquid, altho' finely pencil[']d'. After this damning with faint praise, there follows emphatic rejection in 'the introduction of the House on the embankment destroys all the dignity on the left'. And although the ship seems acceptable to him as being 'happily disposed and color'd', and the sky 'heavy sombre grey … with warm lights (the half tint this leaf)', the crunch comes when, after stating 'the chief light is upon the surge in the foreground – but too much is made to suffer', he concludes 'so that it is artificial – and shows the brown in a more glaring point of v[i]ew and *this* inattention of the forms which waves make upon a lee shore Embanked'.[42]

These remarkably phrased reactions are noteworthy in that they are the comments both of a professional artist and of an Englishman whose terms of reference, at the time, were exclusively English. In Britain 'the forms which waves make upon a lee shore' are inevitably different from those made in Holland, lined as her coasts are with elongated sandbanks. A Dutch fishing-port, moreover, has as a rule a harbour master's house at the end of one of its moles. Turner objected to Ruisdael's composition as well as his execution, yet, in both, the Dutch painter had been true to his typically Dutch subject. As to an actual place called 'Port Ruysdael', this does not exist. The name may have occurred to Turner upon flicking through the pages of old sketchbooks in search of a new subject, as was his habit, and coming across his scribbled 'Sea [gap] Port [gap] Rysdale' at the top of a page instead of 'Seaport' written in one word. Such a genesis would, of course, have been very much in Turner's style.

The last time he had exhibited a seapiece at the Academy was eight years earlier, when he showed 'Entrance of the Meuse'. Now his 'Port Ruysdael' turned out to be the universally praised forerunner of a whole series of seascapes which proved once more his full command of the traditions of Dutch marine art.

Among the pictures produced in the early 1830s there are several 'Van Tromps', representing scenes with the famous seventeenth-century Dutch Admiral Cornelis (or Kornelis) Tromp (1629–91) or his no less renowned father, Admiral Maarten Harpertsz[oon] Tromp (1598–1653) (figs.x, xi). The addition of 'Van' to their surname is only found in England. The father had received a knighthood for escorting Charles I's Queen and the Princess Royal to Amsterdam in order to pawn the crown jewels during the Civil War, and the son had been given a baronetcy for his actions against the Barbary and Dunkirk pirates. Although feared in the Dutch Wars, their name had remained popular, as exemplified in an eighteenth-century song about the broom that the elder 'Van' Tromp reportedly carried at the main of his flagship to indicate his having brushed the enemy from the seas.[43]

The reason for the series must again have been political. The year 1830 saw the outbreak of the Belgian Revolt, when the Whitehall-created Kingdom of the United Netherlands faced disruption and the threat of secession by the Belgian provinces, a situation that in due course drove the Dutch King William I to resort to arms in the so-called 'Belgian Campaign'. Britain not only refused to intervene on his behalf, but in November 1831 a conference of the Great Powers in London imposed an armistice, and in June 1832 they declared Belgium a constitutional monarchy under Leopold of Saxe-Coburg as King. When the Dutch King rejected the conditions of separation, Britain and France impounded Dutch shipping and started a blockade of Dutch ports.

That was the point at which Turner painted 'Admiral Van Tromp's Barge at the Entrance of the Texel 1645' exh.1831

fig.x Engraved by J. Houbraken after Jan Lievens, 'Maarten Harpertszoon Tromp', mezzotint *Private Collection*

fig.xi Engraved by J. Houbraken after Jan Lievens, 'Kornelis Tromp', mezzotint *Private Collection* (no.14). Tromp's miraculous feat in 1645 had been to safe-guard his country's merchant fleet against the depredations of pirate forces. In 1831, stung in particular it would seem, by what was being done to Dutch shipping, Turner would have considered his Government's stance as a form of betrayal; hence, no doubt, more Van Tromp seascapes in 1832 and 1833 (nos.15, 16).

As in the first 'Van Tromp' picture, each of these beautiful seapieces show, in what almost seems a fixed formula, the barge or state yacht of the Admiral returning to flagship or base, 'mission accomplished'. In 'Van Tromp's Shallop at the Entrance of the Scheldt' exh.1832 (no.15), artistic licence is once again in evidence in the shape of the central vessel's hull, in her wearing an odd assortment of flags, and in Tromp's 'shallop'.[44] This shallop is shown flying a big, crested white flag, while the Admiral in his curious headgear is presumably being rowed ashore.

As paintings, the Van Tromp pictures were highly praised in the press, although the reviewer in the *Spectator* found Turner's seas 'not lucid enough', although he added 'But then how airy and tender his distances; still, how perfect the keeping, how pure the colouring!'[45] Possibly Turner came across the anonymous *Vie de Corneille Tromp* (1694) – a *Life*, published in English in 1697 – from his patron William Beckford's library, auctioned in 1823, and he may have seen Backhuysen's 'Embarkation of Van Tromp' at Apsley House in London.

In 1832, still preoccupied with Anglo-Dutch history, Turner seems at the same time prompted by his Whig sympathies. In fact, he did not remain with his Dutch Admiral but went one better and also painted the splendidly dramatic 'The Prince of Orange, William III, Embarked from Holland, and Landed at Torbay, November 4th, 1688, after a Stormy Passage (no.18). Here, the historical background was the Bloodless Revolution of 1688 in which the Roman-Catholic King James II was replaced by the Protestant Prince William III of Orange jointly with his spouse, the Princess Mary. It is interesting to note that, while confusing the date of the landing (the fleet anchored on the 5th, not on the 4th of November which was William and Mary's wedding day in 1677, whereupon he had sailed home in the Royal yacht *Mary*), Turner should have specifically added 'after a stormy passage'. Actually, although William had been blown back by bad storms at a first attempt in October, the expedition had been favoured by an ideal north-easterly (at once dubbed the Prince's 'Protestant Wind').

As to the landing itself, here the painter again used a good deal of imagination. No boat or barge of a seventeenth-century Dutch warship would have an elaborately sculptured and gilded bow *à l'anglaise*, even in a Britain-bound invasion-fleet. Nor had the Prince sailed in 'a yacht', that was 'finally wrecked on Hamburgh sands', as Turner printed in his catalogue entry,[46] but in the new frigate *Den Briel*. And the

William-figure in the stern-sheets would not wear an eighteenth-century three-cornered hat, any more than he would be able to remain upright in such a heavy swell while solemnly lifting his hat in salute to cheering spectators.

'The Prince of Orange ... Landed at Torbay' must have been produced to recall the extent to which Turner's Britain was indebted to former Dutch initiative, as expressed in Thomson's still popular poem *Liberty*.[47] It is also conceivable that Turner's 'stormy passage' in the title echoed the 'heavy passage' through Parliament of the Reform Bill which was so much in the spirit of the Glorious Revolution championed by Turner's late-lamented friend Walter Fawkes. A confused association of thought, on the one hand between William's wedding date and the date of his landing, and, on the other, between the vessel in which he sailed home after the wedding and the one in which he led the invasion fleet seems evident – especially when in 1827 a similar confusion prompted a widely publicised influx of Williamite souvenir hunters into Newcastle where an exceptionally old ship, alleged to have been William's *Mary*, was finally broken up, having been ignominiously sold in the eighteenth century, reclassified as a trader, and subsequently stranded.[48]

'The Prince of Orange ... Landed at Torbay', was not the only picture to remind viewers of 1688. Turner's mistakes may have been based both on a poem he had long loved and on a confused association of thought, but his intentions were consistent. This is endorsed by the fact that in the same exhibition of 1832 he also showed 'Helvoetsluys; – the City of Utrecht, 64, Going to Sea' (no.19). With her sixty-four guns, one of the same invasion fleet's three flagships (that of the squadron of Lt-Admiral Philips van Almonde), she is represented leaving her home base of Hellevoetsluis (a port mentioned in the 'Itinerary Rhine Tour' sketchbook[49]) in order to join on station William's English(!) Admiral-General.

Where the colourful portrayal of William's landing was almost gleefully histrionic, the 'Helvoetsluys' was grey and subdued. As such it became the source of an anecdote about the buoy in its foreground. This story has it that, vexed by the brilliant effect of the flags in Constable's 'Opening of Waterloo Bridge' (Tate Gallery) – which had been hung, as he only discovered on Varnishing Day, next to his own 'Helvoetsluys', Turner marched off, returned with his palette and brush, put a round daub of red lead on his grey sea and shaped it into a buoy. Constable is afterwards reported as saying 'He has been here, and fired a gun'. The irony is that, in the waters between Hellevoetsluis and the shore of the island of Goeree opposite William's base, there is still a line of red (and green) buoys today.

In the year following these pictures, another London Convention agreed to the lifting of the maritime embargo on Dutch shipping, but at the same time to maintain the status quo in Belgium – which was to last until 1839, when the end of the 'United' Netherlands became a legal fact. In 1833

Turner painted 'Van Tromp Returning after the Battle off the Dogger Bank' (no.16). Although an eminently 'Dutch' sea-piece, it was criticised for its painter having got his dates wrong – which was not the case, since there were two Dogger Bank engagements, one in July 1652 and one in 1781, the earlier starting the First Dutch War, the latter belonging to the Fourth (and last). In both battles the Dutch fleet had to retreat, though unbeaten, which was considered a great achievement – and may have been recollected in connection with the position of the Dutch King.

It is difficult to ascertain how far the British public was aware of the historical role of Holland. But it seems doubtful whether Turner would ever have produced this Dutch series – and gone on with it – if the *Athenaeum* had been right in commenting on 'The Prince of Orange … Landing': 'The painter has made this picture somewhat poetical: he has squandered the finest hues and the finest perspective upon a subject which has lost somewhat of its feverish interest in the hearts of Englishmen.'[50]

While still very much in the Dutch orbit, Turner next painted 'The Rotterdam Ferry Boat' exh.1833 (no.20) and '[Antwerp;] Van Goyen Looking Out for a Subject' 1833 (no.21). Both emphatically 'poetical', the two could well be seen as companion pieces. They have a similar composition, almost the same measurements and, for their town profiles, both lean heavily on the sketchbooks from his tour of 1817, that is, on the 'Dort' sketchbook, and the 'Waterloo and Rhine' sketchbook.

Each, however, has another peculiarity. In the 'Rotterdam Ferry Boat', with its light-suffused background dominated by the Church of St Lawrence, it is that on the far right there is a seventeenth-century man-of-war with gun ports open and guns run out. It was probably this that later gave rise to the idea that it was another Van Tromp picture with the Admiral again in a small boat in the foreground and his flagship anchored behind him. But, as Turner would have known, in harbour a serving Admiral would never have himself conveyed in a diminutive sailing boat, and without his flag. The point of the picture may well be the situation of the boatload of civilian passengers – women and children, at that – in their unpretentious little craft between, on one side, a big merchantman bearing down on them and, on the other, an impressive, historicised man-of-war at anchor, while they themselves are in perfect safety crossing the river alongside what to the British was by now the Northern Netherland's chief commercial port.

The oddly titled '[Antwerp;] Van Goyen Looking Out for a Subject' (no.21) presents another mystery. 'Antwerp' was not part of the original title, but some of the principal buildings of that city appear unmistakably in the background. We know that the Dutch Master did indeed visit Antwerp which, before Rotterdam's rise, was the Southern Netherlands' chief commercial port. Van Goyen's aim would no doubt have

fig.xii 'Fishmarket, Rotterdam', engraving by W. Floyd after J.M.W. Turner *Algemeen Rijksarchief, Afdeling Kaarten en Tekeningen, The Hague*

been the same as that of his nineteenth-century English counterpart who was also always on the lookout for suitable harbour views. The well-documented, sunny city-scape in the picture, as in the 'Rotterdam Ferry Boat', is perfectly convincing. Only, some details of the vessel – her heavy rubbing-strakes and the 'Van G' on her stern – are as implausible as the lavishly plumed hat worn by her principal passenger. As panoramas, however, of the two principal Dutch-speaking river-ports teeming with shipping, both pictures are superb.

For several years after this explosion of marines there was silence on Turner's Dutch front until, in August 1840, he once more travelled to Rotterdam and up the Rhine, now on his way to Venice. On this journey he used the 'Rotterdam to Venice' sketchbooks. Then, in the months of August 1841 and July 1842, new trips to Switzerland followed, starting each time at Rotterdam or Ostend. The 'Rotterdam' and 'Rotterdam and Rhine' sketchbooks probably belong to these years.[51] The Dutch drawings in all these sketchbooks, in particular those of sites and shipping at Rotterdam and Dordrecht, provide an almost uninterrupted eye-witness account of everyday life in nineteenth-century Holland; with their greatly varying styles, they, like the earlier ones, further enrich the record.

There were no other 'Dutch' canvases until 1844, when Turner produced three singularly informative Dutch-inspired marines. In 'Van Tromp, Going About to Please his Masters, Ships a Sea, Getting a Good Wetting' (no.17) he used Dutch history again to make a political point. It was to be the last time. His addition to the entry in the exhibition catalogue of 'Vide Lives of the Dutch Painters' may have been meant to suggest an obscure source, but it is a tongue-in-cheek variation on the title of Allan Cunningham's prestigious *Lives of the most Eminent British Painters* of 1829. In the same way, 'ships a Sea' may have been intended to puzzle viewers unfamiliar with the nautical expression 'to ship' for 'to take water over the side'; they would otherwise have imagined that 'a' should have been 'at'.

The picture itself refers to the conflict between Admirals Michiel de Ruyter and Cornelis Tromp, the latter having been accused of leaving his senior colleague in the lurch during the Two Days' Battle with the English of August 1666 in order to pursue some enemy warships with his own squadron. As a result, he was relieved of his command, which in turn made him decide to quit the service altogether. But in 1673 Prince William III, Supreme Commander of the Dutch Forces, succeeded in persuading Tromp to swallow his pride, make his submission to the States General, and serve his beleaguered country again in her hour of need.

What the painter seems to imply in the depiction of his maverick star's 'going about' (i.e. going on a new tack), was that in a national crisis this, and this alone, is the attitude that a great leader should adopt with the powers that be; and Turner, who was subsequently to honour Wellington in 'The Hero of a Hundred Fights' 1847 (Tate Gallery, B&J 427), may, possibly, have been thinking of the crabbed old hero.

The picture was much praised in spite of several anachronistic details. These include a nineteenth-century captain's burgee with initials (at the gaff of Tromp's seventeenth-century vessel), the Admiral's white costume rather than the customary Dutch Calvinist black, and his holding on to the mainstay while unceremoniously waving his hat at 'his Masters', the Members of the States General, in their remarkably steady state barge. It was nevertheless seen as another testimony to Turner's excellence as a marine artist, especially in rendering manoeuvres under sail in turbulent seas.

This leaves two other 'Dutch' pictures of 1844: 'Fishing Boats Bringing a Disabled Ship into Port Ruysdael' (no.22) and 'Ostend' (no.23). Seventeen years after his first 'Port Ruysdael' (1827), the painter returned to his original notes of 1802 on the great Master from Haarlem. At the same time, his mind was also once more occupied with his fisher-folk. Both this picture and 'Ostend' were painted in Turner's later, supremely atmospheric manner. No longer is it purely a sensation of Sublimity that he undertook to impress upon the viewer: in the 'Disabled Ship', a 'sublime' catastrophe has apparently been avoided (the ship's damage remains unspecified), and in the 'Ostend' the sailboat at the centre will evidently succeed in clearing the dangerous pier on her lee and, by the timely gybe of her mainsail, as portrayed, follow the other boats. In fact, in each of these two pictures the mood seems one of defiant determination to survive – albeit in full awareness of the immensity of the forces of nature.

In both pictures, then, Turner might be assumed to have imagined himself returning, in his inevitably approaching decline, to his artistic roots. The bringing of a 'disabled ship' into a safe haven would in that case be an allegory for the age-ing Turner's idea of countering the waning of his creative powers, the name 'Port Ruysdael' symbolising the art of the Dutch Golden Age of which he had confessed so many years ago: 'That made me a painter'.

With 'Ostend', although by then the city was no longer within the territory of the Kingdom of the Netherlands, the pursuit of the broader 'Dutch connection' in his life has come, so to speak, full circle: it was at Ostend that, on 12 August 1817, he first set foot on what at the time was Dutch soil and afterwards he had since passed through the port many times.[52] It seems fitting that with 'Ostend', precisely because Dutch influence had by now been absorbed so completely that it can no longer be singled out, the curtain comes down on this aspect of Turner's incomparable offering.

The truth of Reynolds's exhortation about the need for aspiring painters to 'go to the Dutch School' has never been demonstrated more conclusively. There is many a reference to Dutch Masters in the lectures Turner gave as the Royal Academy's Professor of Perspective in his middle years.[53] Unlike some of his most discerning contemporaries, he never vented any strident irritation – as did Ruskin[54] – or merely thinly disguised disapproval with regard to the Dutch marine painters for their astonishing nautical expertise. An illuminating sentence from one of Turner's lectures to students of the Royal Academy reveals how highly he esteemed the work of Aelbert Cuyp, and is strikingly apt in relation to his own. It reads: 'But Cuyp … knew where to blend minutiae in all the golden colour of ambient vapour.'[55]

One day, exasperated by an unfeeling client who had complained that the picture by Turner that he had acquired was too indistinct, he emphatically retorted: 'Indistinctness is my fault'.[56] By now, it may not be too bold to assert that in these last pictures his 'fault' had in turn been blended 'in all the golden colour' of Dutch 'ambient vapour' and thereby turned into a triumph.

Epilogue

Between 1807 when he was elected Professor of Perspective at the Royal Academy and January 1811 when he began his annual courses of six lectures, Turner undertook extensive research for them. In every course until 1828 when he terminated his appointment there were references to, or actual comments on, Dutch art. Starting with Rembrandt who after Van de Velde had been foremost among the Dutch Masters to influence Turner, it was certainly through Reynolds that this influence had been channelled. Reynolds was both the eighteenth-century's subtlest critic of Rembrandt and his most eloquent admirer. In his opening lecture Turner had touchingly expressed his lasting gratitude to Sir Joshua's inspiration.[57]

Anticipating Keats's idea of 'negative capability' by seven years, Turner declared of Rembrandt's 'Landscape with the Rest on the Flight into Egypt' in a lecture of 1811 that he had 'in no picture … seen that freshness, that negative quality of shade and colour, that aerial perspective enwrapped in gloom ever attempted but by the daring hand of Rembrandt'. Written nine years after his moderately harsh criticisms[58] in his 'Studies in the Louvre' sketchbook, this was undoubtedly his 'most profound verbal tribute' to Rembrandt, as Michael Kitson has observed.[59] It occurred in the same lecture in which he singled out two other landscapes for analysis, stating that

> Rembrandt depended upon his chiaroscuro, his bursts of light and darkness to be felt. He threw a mysterious doubt over the meanest piece of Common [= vulgarity]; nay, more … over each ['The Mill' and 'The Three Trees'] he has thrown that veil of matchless colour, that lucid interval of Morning dawn and dewy light on which the Eye dwells so completely enthrall'd, and it seeks not for its liberty, but as it were, thinks it a sacrilege to pierce the mystic shell of colour in search of form.[60]

After 'The Field of Waterloo' with its several very Rembrandtesque aspects, such as an extraordinary handling of various light-sources and an unusually effective colouring of the massed bodies perceived in semi-darkness, Turner tended to allow the sun to take pride of place in his pictures, marking its position in many of his landscape sketches.

On another tack, a very different statement reads: 'Without affecting to do anything, Teniers has given us that individuality, which the great genius of Rubens in his Flemish Fete and pastorals always seem'd in search of'.[61] To what extent Turner's use of Teniers-like groups bears out this statement need not be decided here. In a further expression of his feelings about certain Dutch Masters Turner declared:

'Cuyp, Paul Potter and Adrian van der Velde sought for simplicity before commonality which too often regulated their choice and alas their introductions, yet for colour and minuteness of touch of every weed and briar [they] long bore away the palm of labour and execution.'[62] Even today 'colour and minuteness of touch' may still be considered essential ingredients of Reynolds's Dutch 'Grammar School', no matter what the curriculum or tests of its 'Language' programme.

Notes

1. A little later, perhaps somewhat shortsightedly, Reynolds specified 'It is to the eye only that the works of this school are addressed', meaning that, to him, Dutch painting dealt mainly with the world known through the sense of sight rather than through the intellect. Joshua Reynolds, *Works … Containing the Discourses … [and] A Journey to Flanders and Holland…* (4th ed. 1809, 3 vols., vol.II, pp.359–64).

2. For the historical details see E.H. Kossmann, *The Low Countries, 1780–1940*, 1978, pp.103–95.

3. The British Institution for Promoting the Fine Arts was an association, founded in 1805, which offered prizes, bought modern works, and held two annual exhibitions, one of contemporary British painting and (from 1816) one of Old Masters. In its exhibition catalogue of 6 March 1815, the directors gave notice that, in the ensuing year, instead of a prize for History or Landscape Painting, they have 'set apart One Thousand Guineas … for finished Sketches, illustrative of, or connected with, the Successes of the British Army … such Sketches to be painted in Oil' (British Institution, exh. cat., 1815, p.I.)

4. A.G.H. Bachrach, 'The Field of Waterloo and Beyond', *Turner Studies*, vol.I, no.2, 1981, pp.4–11.

5. Cecilia Powell, *Turner's Rivers of Europe: The Rhine, Meuse and Mosel*, exh. cat., Tate Gallery 1991, p.11 and passim.

6. TB CLIX 100.

7. Walter Thornbury, *The Life and Correspondence of J.M.W. Turner*, 1862, rev. ed. 1877, p.8. The mezzotint was engraved by Elisha Kirkall and printed in green ink in 1724 (A.G.H. Bachrach, 'Turner's Holland', *Dutch Quarterly Review*, vol.6, no.2, 1976, p.88).

8. Francis Egerton, 3rd and last Duke of Bridgewater (1736–1803), visited Holland when on his Grand Tour in 1753, subsequently developed his coalmines in Lancashire, and then took the initiative for (and actually financed throughout) the construction of canals such as the one connecting Liverpool and Manchester, for the transport of coal and, to a lesser extent, even of passengers.

9. Frank Herrmann, *The English as Collectors*, 1972, pp.137–9.

10. This phenomenon constituted the theme of the Anglo–Dutch exhibition in 1971, entitled *Shock of Recognition* (see A.G.H. Bachrach, *Schok der Herkenning/Shock of Recognition*, exh. cat., Mauritshuis, The Hague, and Tate Gallery, London 1971).

11. See, for example, D'Oench, in C. White, D. Alexander and E. D'Oench, *Rembrandt in Eighteenth Century England*, 1983, p.63.

12. A.J. Finberg, *The Life of J.M.W. Turner*, 1961 (2nd ed.), p.71, and Michael Kitson, 'Turner and Rembrandt', *Turner Studies*, vol.8, no.1, 1988, pp.2–19.

13. Finberg 1961, chap.x, 'Studies in the Louvre', p.90; also below, p.47.

14. L. Herrmann, *Turner's Prints*, 1990, p.62. See also pp.24–72 for the vicissitudes of the *Liber*'s production for teaching exercises in the different categories of landscape – which Turner called History, Mountains, Pastoral, Marine, Architecture, and Epic Pastoral – and for the drawn-out publication history of this series of engravings, which was started in 1807 and abandoned in 1819.

15. Thomas Paine, in *The Age of Reason* (1795, Pt.II, p.20), first formulated this idea which Turner appears gleefully to have adopted ('Cockermouth' sketchbook, TB CX 1). See also, from a different angle, Andrew Wilton, 'Sublime or Ridiculous?', *New Literary History*, vol.16, 1984/5, pp.343–76.

16. Jerrold Ziff, 'Turner on Poetry and Painting', *Studies in Romanticism*, 1964, vol.III, p.198.

17. John Gage, *J.M.W. Turner: A Wonderful Range of Mind*, 1987, p.111.

18. This threat was only finally lifted in the autumn of the following year, after Napoleon turned to attack Austria and the French fleet was annihilated at Trafalgar. Compare Coleridge's *Fears in Solitude*, written in 1798.

19. *Sun*, 10 May 1804, as in B&J, p.34. The paper even declared 'Why the scene … should be placed so far back as in 1665, it is difficult to conceive except by referring to the affectation which almost invariably appears in the work of the Artist. There is nothing in the subject to excite an interest.'

20. Turner to Sir John Fleming Leicester, 16 Dec. 1810, with a minute pen-sketch (Gage, *Collected Correspondence*, 1980, p.44).

21. Constable to Fisher, 23 Oct. 1821 (R.B. Beckett, *John Constable's Correspondence*, 1962–9, vol.VI, p.77).

22. Gage 1987, p.145.

23. The full text was:
    Aid me, ye Powers! O bid my thoughts to roll
    In quick succession, animate my soul;
    Descend my Muse, and every thought refine,
    And finish well my long, my *long-sought* line.

24. In 1817 the charge for the crossing from Harwich to Hellevoetsluys was £2 14s 6d. The *Times* of 9 Aug. carried on its front page the advertisement 'For Ostend from Botolph Wharf, near London Bridge … Fares best cabin 18s.'

25. 'Lost in the Wallet … Cambells Belgium' ('Itinerary Rhine Tour Sketchbook', TB CLIX 101).

26. A.G.H. Bachrach, 'New Light on Turner's Travel Preparations', *Turner Studies*, vol.11, no.1, 1991, pp.32–5.

27. TB CLIX 1–15.

28. See, for instance, TB CLXII 68 or 92a.

29. Cecilia Powell, 'Turner's Women: The Painted Veil', *Turner Society News*, no.63, 1993, p.14.

30. 'Itinerary Rhine Tour' sketchbook (TB CLIX 10); A.G.H. Bachrach, 'The Field of Waterloo and Beyond', *Turner Studies*, vol.I, no.2, 1981, pp.4–11; J. Ziff, 'Turner as Defender of the Art between 1810–20', *Turner Studies*, vol.8, no.2, 1988, pp.13–25.

31. The verses Turner printed in the RA catalogue were Canto III, stanza 28.

32. In the *Examiner*, 24 May 1818, Hazlitt recognised 'the magical illustration of how at night-fall there was only left the fiery explosions and carnage after the battle, when the wives and brothers and sons of the slain come, with a anxious eyes and agonized hearts, to look at Ambition's charnel-house.'

33. In *The Annals of the Fine Arts* (see B&J, p.93). For an assessment of the Turner–Byron relationship, see David Blayney Brown, *Turner and Byron*, exh. cat., Tate Gallery 1992, pp.28–32.

34. David Blayney Brown, *Augustus Wall Callcott*, exh.cat., Tate Gallery 1981, p.78.

35. TB CLXIV 8. The same 'Guards' sketchbook also has a good deal of material for 'Raby Castle' (B&J 136). If the anecdotal element of the fox-hunt is skipped, the painting of the background landscape and the sky does recall the painter's recent experience of Dutch light.

36. TB CLXII.

37. Finberg 1960, p.291.

38. TB CCXIV and CCXV.

39. A 'Beach at Scheveningen' by Van de Velde is in the National Gallery, London, and Simon de Vlieger's 'Scheveningen' is in the National Maritime Museum, Greenwich.

40. Turner had possibly remembered Reynolds's *Journey to Flanders and Holland*, which recorded having seen 'Two [pictures] … by Terburch, the white satin remarkably well painted. He seldom omitted to introduce a piece of white satin in his pictures' (p.360). For the central place of 'The Parental Visit' in Terborch's oeuvre, see S.J. Gudlaugsson's studies and J.P. Guepin's essay in *Gerard Terborch*, exh.cat., Mauritshuis, The Hague 1974, pp.19–23, 25–9, 31–8.

41. Sketched copies are in TB LXXII 50a, 61; analyses on pp.60 and 60a.

42. Ibid.

43. 'Tie a broom to the mast', said he,
    For a broom is the sign for me,
    That wherever I go,
    The world may know,
    I sweep the mighty sea.
    (*Popular Songs*, a nineteenth-century collection)

44. In maritime usage, 'shallop' is not only the name for a small sailing boat but also for a skiff.

45. *Spectator*, 12 May 1832.

46. Turner's text read: 'The yacht in which his Majesty sailed was, after many changes and services, finally wrecked on Hamburgh sands.'

47. *Liberty*, 1738, Pt.IV, lines 1117–23.

48. See the *Newcastle Courant* of 24 February and 3 March 1827, and W. Senior, 'The Legend of the "Betsy Cains" [the ship's new name], *Mariner's Mirror*, vol.I, no.1, 1911, pp.40–4. There was one more *Mary*; the yacht in which Princess Mary came over in 1689 for the coronation, will have added to the confusion.

49. TB CLIX reads on p.13a:
    'Helvoutsluys. Sluice dam 80 feet water
    Brill to Rotterdam 12 Miles 2 ducats
        4 pence[?]
    Scheedam 6 WSW Maesluce
    Statue of Erasmus by Keiser Boomquay
    Dort 12 Miels [*sic*] Maese calld the Merwe.
    Gorcum 12½

Dlft 6 Mil. from the Hague 9 from R
  Vijverburg and Palace in the Wood
  Scheveling 2
Leyden 9 miles from Hague in the town
  House
a paintg of the Judgement by Lucas de
  Leyde
Haerlem 10 Miles from Amsterdam'
In both Hills and Campbell the sources of
these notes are to be found towards the end of
their books, Campbell being the most detailed
(see *The Traveller's Complete Guide*, 1817,
pp.223–4 and *Sketches in Flanders and Holland*,
1816, p.202).
[50] *Athenaeum*, 26 May 1832.
[51] TB CCCXX, CCCXXI and CCCXXII.
[52] There are later sketches marked 'Ostend' in
the 'Ostend, Rhine and Wurzburg' sketchbook (TB CCCIII 6a, 17, 19, 21) as also in
'Miscellaneous Black and White Drawings'
(TB CCCXLIV 310).
[53] Turner was elected to this Chair on 10
December 1807; his first lecture was given on
7 January 1811. See for Turner's thoughts in
this context, Maurice Davies, *Turner as
Professor*, exh. cat., Tate Gallery 1992.
[54] 'I can perceive nothing in Vandevelde or
Backhuysen of the lowest redeeming merit: no
power, no presence of intellect, or evidence of
perception of any sort or kind, no resem-
blance, even the feeblest, of anything natural,
no invention, even the most sluggish, of anything agreeable …; though I can understand
why people admire everything else in the old
art … when I find they can even *endure* the
sight of a Backhuysen on their room walls … it
makes me hopeless at once …; I can trace the
evil influence of Vandevelde on most of his
[Turner's] early sea-painting (*Modern Painters*,
1989 ed., vol.I, pt.II, p.138).
[55] See Jerrold Ziff, '"Backgrounds: Introduction
of Architecture and Landscape": A Lecture by
J.M.W. Turner', *Journal of the Warburg and Cour-
tauld Institutes*, vol.26, 1963, p.146.
[56] The line occurs in Turner's correspondence
with Leslie in 1845 about the buyer of 'Staffa,
Fingall's Cave', painted in 1832 (Finberg 1961,
p.336).
[57] 'I cannot look back but with pride and pleasure to that time, the halcyon perhaps of my
days, when I … listen'd … with a just sense
and respect towards the institution and its
then President Sir Joshua Reynolds, whose
Discourses must yet be warm in many a recollection.' (Turner, 'Backgrounds', as in Ziff
1963, p.125, n.8).
[58] In 1802 he noted: 'The Good Samaritan at
the Iron Door – rather monotonous being
painted [on] a brown (asphaltum) ground
which pervades thro' the sky. The lights are
spotty and the Breadth lies in the half tone
viz: upon the wall, even the colouring of the
figures are of the same for the Samaritan only
can be seen colour'd in yellow and the Boys
cap Red, the jacket grey, the man next
stronger and the Traveller a Dark brown and
… the boy greenish and the woman with the
L.cap' (TB LXXII 60).
[59] Kitson 'Turner and Rembrandt', p.7.
[60] As in Ziff 1963, p.146.
[61] Turner is referring here to 'The Flemish Mar-
riage Feast' at Louther Castle (Ziff, 1963,
p.146). Eric Shanes has pointed out a possible

model in this picture for the man seen from
behind in Turner's 'Sun Rising through
Vapour' (Shanes, *Turner's Human Landscape*,
pp.315–16) – although fishermen in red knitted
caps abound in Dutch and Flemish pictures,
as they do in Turner's.
[62] See Ziff 1963.

Places in Holland in Turner's Sketchbooks

(relevant sketchbooks are given in round
brackets)

Abcoude ('Dort')
Amstel ('Dort'; 'Holland')
Amsterdam ('Itinerary Rhine Tour'; 'Dort';
  'Holland')
Antwerp ('Itinerary Rhine Tour'; 'Dort')
Arnhe[i]m ('Rotterdam and Rhine'; 'Arnheim')
Biesbos[ch] ('Holland')
Breda ('Holland, Meuse and Cologne')
Den Briel [Brill] ('Holland')
Bruges ('Itinerary Rhine Tour'; 'Waterloo and
  Rhine'; 'Holland'; 'Rhine, Meuse and
  Moselle')
Brussels ('Itinerary Rhine Tour'; 'Waterloo and
  Rhine'; 'Meuse and Moselle'; 'Brussels to
  Mannheim')
Delft ('Holland'; 'Rotterdam and Rhine')
Dordrecht [Dort] ('Dort'; 'Rotterdam')
Flushing ('Rotterdam, Flushing and Lausanne')
Ghent ('Itinerary Rhine Tour'; 'Waterloo and
  Rhine'; 'Holland')
Goeree ('Rotterdam')
Haarlam ('Dort')
Den Haag [The Hague] ('Dort')
Helvoetsluys ('Itinerary Rhine Tour')
Huy ('Meuse and Moselle')
Katwijk ('Dort')
Laeken ('Brussels to Mannheim')
Leiden ('Holland')
Luik [Liège] ('Meuse and Moselle')
Loenersloot ('Holland')
Leuven [Louvain] ('Holland, Meuse and
  Cologne')
Maassluis [Maesensluys] ('Holland')
Maastricht ('Holland')
Moerdijk [Moredyke] ('Rotterdam')
Namen [Namur] ('Itinerary Rhine Tour'; 'Dort';
  'Meuse and Moselle'; 'Spa, Dinant and
  Namur')
Nieuwpoort [Newport] ('Holland')
Nieuwedam [Newendam] ('Holland')
Ostend ('Itinerary Rhine Tour'; 'Holland';
  'Ostend, Rhine and Wurzburg'; 'Ostend,
  Rhine and Berne')
Rotterdam ('Itinerary Rhine Tour'; 'Waterloo
  and Rhine'; 'Dort'; 'Holland'; 'Rotterdam';
  'Rotterdam and Rhine')
Scheveningen ('Dort')
Schiedam [Sheedam] ('Dort')
Utrecht ('Dort')
Waterloo ('Itinerary Rhine Tour'; 'Waterloo and
  Rhine'; 'Dort')
Issel [Essel] ('Rotterdam and Rhine')

Turner's Sketchbooks with Dutch Place Names

1817 'Itinerary Rhine Tour' (TB CLIX)
1817 'Waterloo and Rhine' (TB CLX)
1817 'Dort' (TB CLXII)
1825 'Holland' (TB CCXIV)
1826 'Holland, Meuse and Cologne' (TB CCXV)
1826 'Meuse and Moselle' (TB CCXVI)
1826 'Huy and Dinant' (TB CCXVII)
1834 'Oxford and Bruges' (TB CCLXXXVI)
1834 'Spa, Dinant and Namur' (TB CCLXXXVII)
1839 'Brussels to Mannheim' (TB CCXCVI)
1839 'Ostend, Rhine and Warzburg' (TB CCCIII)
1840 'Rotterdam to Venice' (TB CCCXX)
1840 'Rotterdam' (TB CCCXXI)
1840 'Rotterdam and Rhine' (TB CCCXXII)
1840 'Arnheim' (TB CCCXXIV)
1841 'Rhine, Flushing and Lausanne'
  (TB CCCXXX)
1844 'Ostend, Rhine and Berne' (TB CCCXXVII)

Further Reading

Campbell, Charles, *The Traveller's Complete Guide
through Belgium and Holland*, 1815, revised 1817

Gage, John, *J.M.W. Turner: 'A Wonderful Range of
Mind'*, 1987

Herrmann, Luke, *Turner Prints: The Engraved Work
of J.M.W. Turner*, 1990

Hills, Robert, *Sketches in Flanders and Holland*, 1816

Kossman, E.H., *The Low Countries, 1780–1940*,
1978

Shanes, Eric, *Turner's Human Landscape*, 1990

Wilton, Andrew, *The Life and Work of J.M.W.
Turner*, 1979 (catalogue of watercolours)

Turner's Holland

Explanatory Note

Unless otherwise stated, works are by J.M.W. Turner. Measurements are given in centimetres, followed by inches in brackets, height before width. Items included in the exhibition are marked with an asterisk.

All works by Turner in the Tate Gallery Collection were bequeathed by the artist in 1856.

Abbreviations

B&J Martin Butlin and Evelyn Joll, *The Paintings of J.M.W. Turner*, 2 vols., revised edition 1984

R W.G. Rawlinson, *The Engraved Work of J.M.W. Turner, R.A.*, 2 vols., 1908 and 1913

TB A.J. Finberg, *A Complete Inventory of the Drawings of the Turner Bequest*, 2 vols., 1909

1 Dutch Boats in a Gale; Fishermen Endeavouring to Put their Fish on Board (The Bridgewater Seapiece) exh.1801

Oil on canvas 162.5 × 222 (64 × 87½)
On loan to the National Gallery, London, from a Private Collection, England
B&J 14

Commissioned by the Duke of Bridgewater as a pendant to the younger Willem Van de Velde's 'A Rising Gale' (fig.1b), Turner's composition was the outcome of a series of studies in the 'Calais Pier' sketchbook (TB LXXXI 104–5, 129 and figs.1c–f). These reveal how carefully the artist analysed the various elements in the Dutch seapiece. However, he would already have been well acquainted with the type of vessels depicted; Dutch boats were a familiar sight in the Thames estuary, and he used to travel by barge to visit his relatives in Margate.

In 'A Rising Gale', on the left of the picture ominous clouds cast a dark shadow on the sea. To the right is a beurtschip (Dutch packet-boat), close-hauled on the starboard-tack in a strong south-easterly. Turner evidently did not want simply to

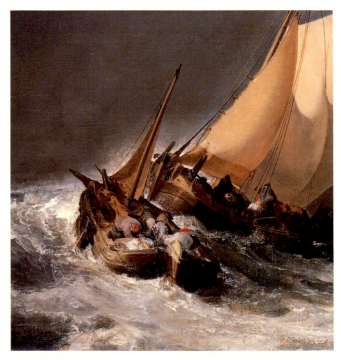

fig.1a Detail

produce a mirror-image of 'A Rising Gale'. He kept a clear parallelism in his sky, which forms a dark focus of attention when the picture is hung to the right of the Van de Velde. But he also wanted to be original, and achieved this by introducing eighteenth-century Burkean 'Sublimity' (see p.12) in the near-catastrophe at the heart of the picture (fig.1a). The fishing boats are obviously on a collision course; the sense of danger is heightened by the unawareness of the crew in the smaller vessel, busy gathering their catch into baskets for the big smacks to take ashore. Only by backing his jib could the helmsman avoid a crash, but the wind needed for this manoeuvre is in any case stolen by the bulging sails of the other boats. The marked diagonals of light and dark, consistently combined with the pattern of masts and spars, imply the contrast between present peril and distant safety.

The huge success of this picture in the Royal Academy exhibition in 1801 was achieved in spite of scathing remarks by connoisseurs such as Sir George Beaumont who declared 'Vandervelde's [sic] picture made Turner's sea appear like pease soup'. But Benjamin West, the then President of the Royal Academy commented: 'What Rembrandt thought of but could not do'.

See also p.12, above.

fig.1b Willem Van de Velde the Younger, 'A Rising Gale', 1671–2
The Toledo Museum of Art; Purchased with Funds from the Libbey Endowment, Gift of Edward Drummond Libbey

fig.1c TB LXXXI 118–19

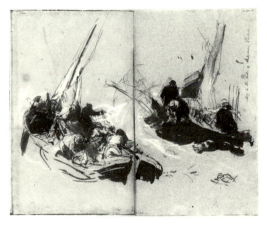

fig.1d TB LXXXI 126–7

fig.1e TB LXXXI 122–3

fig.1f TB LXXXI 106–7

2 Calais Pier, with French Poissards Preparing for Sea; An English Packet Arriving exh.1803*

Oil on canvas 172 × 240 (63¾ × 94½)
Trustees of the National Gallery, London
B&J 24

This painting, the outcome of Turner's first Continental visit, was immediately recognised as being painted according to the best traditions of Dutch seascapes in the Ruisdael and Backhuysen manner. Preliminary studies in the 'Calais Pier' sketchbook (TB LXXXI) reveal an intriguing line of thought before the final idea for the picture was conceived and its definitive composition reached.

Various motifs went into the picture's overall design. Next to the 'Sublime' – the near-collision at the centre (fig.2a, and fig.ii on p.14), as in 'Dutch Boats in a Gale' (no.1) – he introduced another element, that of the 'Ridiculous' (reputed to be only one step away from the 'Sublime'). This is embodied in the altercation between the inept fishermen, in the right foreground, who are trying to avoid being smashed against the pier, and the fishwife (fig.iii on p.14). Evidently narrative additions to the original concept of an atmospheric harbour

view, these facetious elements lend an ironic overtone to the 'preparing for sea' of the title, with the packet's position symbolic of the perennial difficulties of the British approach to 'Europe'.

It is blowing a fresh south-easterly but the sky is clearing and, as in 'Dutch Boats', the horizon is bathed in sunlight. The rendering of the waves in the foreground is masterly; Sir George Beaumont's criticism likening them to 'veins on a marble slab' merely reveals ignorance.

The notion that 'Calais Pier' depicts a personal experience of the artist is misleading; as relevant leaves in the sketchbook show, he joined impatient fellow-tourists in the ferry's boat, who preferred to be rowed ashore rather than wait on board for the turning of the tide. But the state of the sea was such that they were 'nearly swamped' (fig.2b). Further stages in 'Our situation at Calais' are recorded (TB LXXXI 70, 71, 74), the series as a whole revealing in retrospect how traumatic the experience must have been. After landing on the beach, Turner must have made his way to the harbour to watch his 'English packet arriving' – and observe the locals.

See also pp.13–14, above.

fig.2a TB LXXXI 146

fig.2b TB LXXXI 58–9
Inscribed 'Our landing at Calais – nearly swampt'

3 Fishing Boats Entering Calais Harbour *c.*1803

Oil on canvas 73.7 × 98.4 (29 × 38³⁄₄)

The Frick Collection, New York

B&J 142

Whereas 'Calais Pier' (no.2) shows the harbour entrance viewed from the dock, this picture depicts the entrance from the outer harbour. Again the situation is dangerous – the two Dutch fishing boats will soon be forced to go about to avoid smashing into each other or the pier on their port side, but in doing so they will risk collision with outward-bound vessels.

Weather conditions in the two pictures are identical, as is the red cap worn by a member of each crew. The shouted conversation going on in the nearest vessel is clearly about the boy clinging to the mast and sprit in a senseless attempt to straighten the luff of the mainsail in order to increase speed. He, like the figure pointing in apparent dismay at a big wave they have already safely passed, could well embody the 'Ridiculous'.

The picture was etched and engraved by Turner himself

fig.3a 'Entrance of Calais Harbour' (RL 55; A01116)

(with conditions toned down) for Part XI of his *Liber Studiorum* (fig.3a). Sketches used are in the 'Small Calais Pier' and 'Studies for Pictures' sketchbooks (TB LXXI, TB LXIX).

See also pp.13–14, above.

4 Boats Carrying Out Anchors and Cables to Dutch Men of War, in 1665 *c.*1804
Oil on canvas 101.6 × 130.8 (40 × 51½)
The Corcoran Gallery of Art, Washington, William A. Clark Collection
B&J 52

The first of Turner's politically motivated marines based on episodes in Dutch seventeenth-century history. The message – Government beware, complacency about the country's defences has led to calamity before! – was not generally recognised. Turner wanted to remind viewers that the raid by the Dutch on the Medway in 1667, so disastrous for the English, had been the precise result of underestimating the Dutch capacity to refit after losses at the Battle of Lowestoft in 1665. This should not happen again: in spite of Nelson's early victories Napoleon could still attempt an invasion.

In line with the prevailing tradition in Britain that seawater should be depicted as green and transparent, critics objected, as they had for 'Calais Pier' (no.2), to Turner's style. The *Sun* even sneered: 'the Sea seems to have been painted with *birchbroom* and *whitening*', a criticism in keeping with the objections among certain connoisseurs to what they dubbed the 'White Painters'. But Turner's rendering of turbulent waves seems impeccable.

See also p.14, above.

5 Sun Rising through Vapour; Fishermen Cleaning and Selling Fish exh.1807*

Oil on canvas 134.5 × 179 (53 × 70½)

Trustees of the National Gallery, London

B&J 69

As preliminary studies in the 'Calais Pier' sketchbook indicate (TB LXXXI 24, 26, 34, 40, 56; figs.5b–c), this picture was conceived as a Cuypish sunrise seen from a beach, with boats at anchor in a calm. What was probably the first study (fig.5b), is a fully drawn sketch with a marked diagonal surf-line on the beach but with neither staffage nor pier, and Turner may subsequently have felt it lacked drama. The boats on the left recall Van de Capelle; the man-of-war silhouetted under the orb of the sun is pure Van de Velde (see fig.1b on p.29). In later studies, the number of boats was reduced, and one was drawn on a sheet which at its right had an earlier sketch of a crowded biblical scene, at right-angles to the horizon (TB LXXXI 34). This may have suggested the idea of introducing the fish-market, and so filling the empty triangle of sand in the foreground and balancing the overall composition, as in 'Calais Pier' (no.2).

If this time it is not 'Sublimity', as defined by Edmund Burke, that provides the keynote of the picture, but Burkean 'Beauty' (see p.12), the group of figures on the right (recalling Teniers or Van Ostade), introduces the 'Ridiculous' again, since no Dutch fishing folk would bring jars and glasses onto a beach where business was being transacted at dawn.

Turner also referred to this work as 'Dutch Boats and Fish-Market' and 'Dutch Boats', although not having visited Holland before, his sea coast faces west and so to the Dutch the picture would have to be called 'Sun Setting'. The title 'Dutch Boats' was used in a letter from Turner to Sir John Fleming Leicester, the purchaser, dated 12 December 1810, above a pen and ink illustration of the work (fig.5d). There is also a later version of the picture, dating from 1809 (B&J 95).

See also pp.14–15, above.

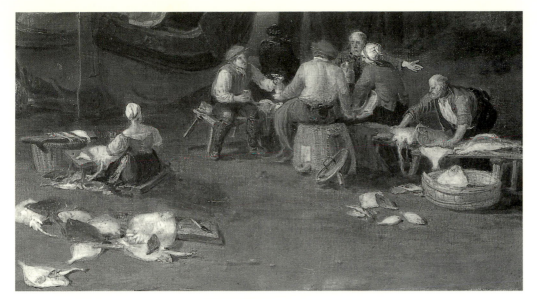

fig.5a Detail

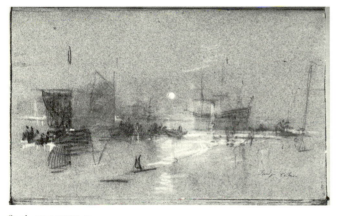

fig.5b TB LXXXI 40

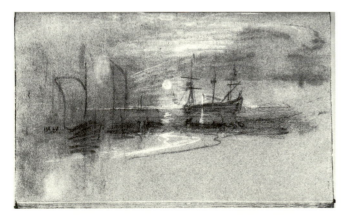

fig.5c TB LXXXI 56

Blythe Sand

Gravesend

Dutch Boats

4 feet long

5 feet

This wants lining and a weeks work

This – 16 feet long / wants cleaning

Queen Ann St West Decr 12 1810

Sir John

Perhaps the above slight mem[o] of the only four subjects I have near the size may lead your recollection in regard to their finish or class. and if [illegible] you would favour me with a call. I would most certainly remain at home

Your most truly obliged

J M W Turner

Dutch Boats, now in 1st [illegible] Gallery

[illegible] Boats

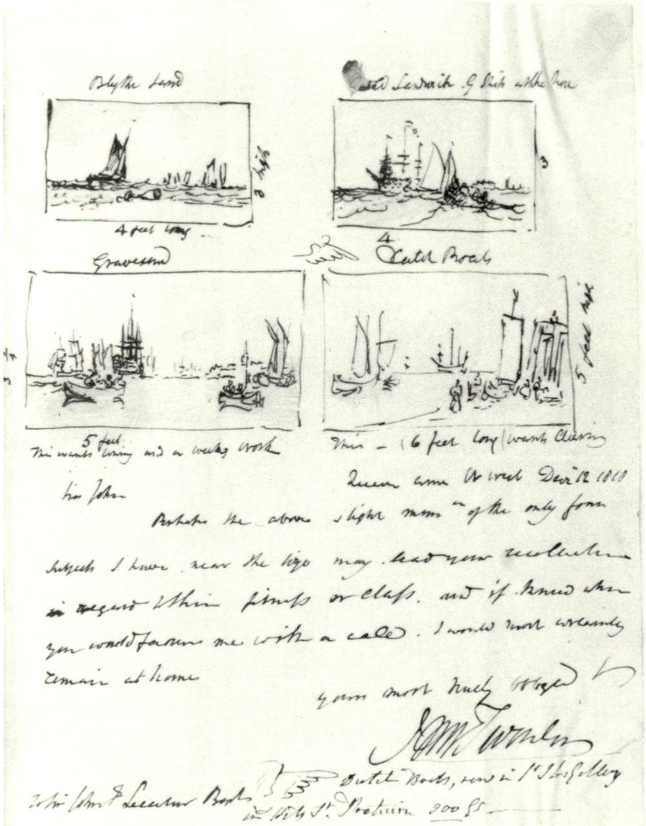

fig.5d Letter showing (bottom right) alternative title: 'Dutch Boats'
Tabley House Collection, Victoria University of Manchester

6 The Unpaid Bill, Or the Dentist Reproving his Son's Prodigality exh.1808

Oil on panel 59.4 × 80 (23⅜ × 31½)

Private Collection

B&J 81

After 'Dutch Boats in a Gale' (no.1) this work was Turner's only other direct pendant to a Dutch Old Master. It was painted for the connoisseur Richard Payne Knight, who wished to show, in a semi-pastiche of another work he owned, 'The Cradle' (subsequently recognised as a Holy Family), thought at the time to be by Rembrandt (fig.6a), that Moderns can stand up to Old Masters. Turner was flattered by the commission and wanted to outshine David Wilkie, one of whose specialities was painting Dutch-inspired genre scenes.

The composition was also intended to express Payne Knight's ideas about the close relationship between the 'Ridiculous' and the 'Sublime', the latter being embodied in Rembrandt's picture, the former in Turner's. In fact, the two pictures present a complete antithesis on the theme of parenthood.

fig.6a School of Rembrandt, 'The Holy Family at Night'
Rijksmuseum, Amsterdam

Preparatory drawings are in the 'River and Margate' sketchbook (TB XCIX 73, 74, 75 verso and 77 verso), and TB CXCV(a) 1. Turner was clearly familiar with the 'Picturesque' qualities in Teniers's subjects of alchemist shops.

See also p.15, above.

7 The Field Of Waterloo exh.1818*

Oil on canvas 147.5 × 238.8 (58 × 94)
Tate Gallery
N00500
B&J 138

One of the main reasons for Turner's tour of 1817 was to visit
the battlefield (which generally gave rise to sentimentally
heroic depiction, as in Allan's later 'Battle of Waterloo'; fig.7c)
in order to record his impressions on the spot. On arrival on
Saturday 16 August, he made nineteen sketches of the field in
the 'Waterloo and Rhine' sketchbook (TB CLX), following the
descriptions of both Robert Hills in his *Sketches in Flanders and
Holland* of 1816 and in Charles Campbell's *Traveller's Guide*
new chapter, of 1817, and, presumably, information from one
of the local farmers.

Making his way south from Waterloo to the battlefield,
Turner drew the fortified farm of La Haye Sainte, which was
lost and then reconquered by the Allies at terrible cost in
human life (fig.7d). It seems likely that someone told Turner
the details of the battle, as he included precise inscriptions
recording what happened. In one sketch (fig.7e), he looks
northwards towards La Haye Sainte along the 'Causeway
down which Bonaparte advanced'. A diagram (top left) shows
the crossroads with the farm in the middle, and the inn on the
extreme left. Another drawing (fig.7f) shows a close view of

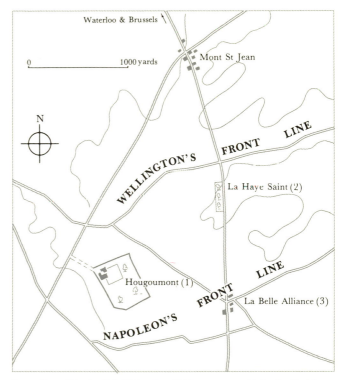

fig.7a Plan of the battlefield showing (1) Hougoumont, (2) the fortified farm
of La Haye Sainte, and (3) the inn of La Belle Alliance

part of the Manor, with a diagram of the 'causeway through the corn', superimposed on the sketch, and a plan of the Manor on the right. Here Turner indicates 'Hollow where the great Carnage took place of the Cuirassiers by the Guards' which became the site of his oil painting. He also drew a view of the Manor House (fig.7g). For his documentation, he made a series of studies of uniforms and accoutrements of a Guards regiment in his 'Guards' sketchbook (TB CLXIV 50 verso and 27; fig.7h). In the same sketchbook he drew two sketches of grieving women (TB CLXIV 7).

Turner's daring, amidst national euphoria, to commemorate the liberation of Europe from French tyranny in a composition of utter desolation and profound grief, was unprecedented, even though it was historically correct in every detail.

The scene, which shows the evening after the battle, is lit by three sources of light: the torches of the women desperately searching for their nearest and dearest in a mound of dead French soldiers and Scots Guards, piled together regardless of rank or allegiance (fig.7b); the burning ruins of Hougo(u)mont Manor, the stronghold on which the outcome of the whole war had hinged; and the flare by which wounded survivors hoped to frighten off ruthless marauders. The whole expressed in every way Byron's passage in Canto III of *Childe Harold*, which, printed in the Academy's catalogue, compressed in only a few verses the harrowing transition from the Duchess of Richmond's glittering officers' ball in Brussels on the evening before the battle to the deadly carnage on the field of Waterloo (see p.17).

See also pp.15–17, above.

fig.7b Detail

fig.7c Sir William Allan, 'Battle of Waterloo', 1843
Board of Trustees of the Victoria and Albert Museum

fig.7d TB CLX 20 verso. Inscribed (l. to r.) 'Causeway', leading to the inn of 'Belle Aliance' [sic], and the farm of 'Haye Sainte'

fig.7g TB CLX 26. Inscribed 'General view of Hugomont from the British lines'

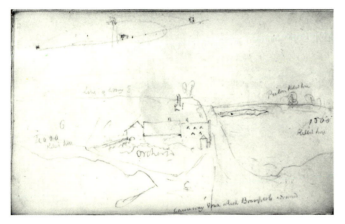

fig.7e TB CLX 21 verso. Inscribed (l. to r.) '4000 killed here', 'Line of Army E[nglish]', 'orchard', 'Picton killed here' and '1500 killed here'

fig.7h TB CLXIV 27

fig.7f TB CLX 24 verso. Inscribed (l. to r.) 'Entrance Gate of Hugomont forced 4 times', 'Picton', 'Causeway to Belle', 'orchard', 'Farm', 'Gate'. (At top:) 'French Line', (at bottom:), 'British Lines'

8 The Field of Waterloo 'Hougoumont' 1819*
Watercolour on paper 28.7 × 38.8 (11¼ × 15¼)
Syndics of the Fitzwilliam Museum, Cambridge

This watercolour represents the same site as Turner's oil
painting (no.7), but without the mound of dead soldiers or the
grieving women. The vignette by William Miller, based on
Turner's sketches from 1817, which appeared in Scott's *Miscellaneous Prose* (1834–6) does not show the aftermath of the
battle; the soldier stands at ease (fig.8a). Another engraving,
by Edward Finden, was published as the title vignette to volume XIV of *Life and Works of Byron*, in 1833, and used again in
Finden's Landscape Illustrations, part XIV. In *Life and Works* it illus-
trates a striking line from *The Age of Bronze* (v.222) – 'Oh,
bloody and most bootless Waterloo!' (fig.8b).

See also p.17, above.

fig.8a 'Hougoumont', 1834 *Private Collection*

fig.8b 'The Field of Waterloo. From Hougemont', 1833 (T06185)

9 Dort or Dordrecht. The Dort Packet-Boat From Rotterdam Becalmed exh.1818

Oil on canvas 157.5 × 233 (62 × 92)

Yale Center for British Art, Paul Mellon Collection

B&J 137

Likewise painted after Turner's return from his first Dutch tour in 1817, the 'Dort' was considered 'one of the most magnificent pictures ever exhibited, and does honour to the age' (*Morning Chronicle*, May 1818). It was bought at once by Walter Fawkes and subsequently recorded in its position at Farnley Hall in a watercolour by Turner (fig.ix on p.19).

The picture represents a perfect amalgam of personal experience (even the weather is meteorologically correct) and the Dutch Golden Age tradition embodied by Aelbert Cuyp, whose 'The Maas at Dordrecht' (fig.vii on p.17) had been exhibited at the British Institution in 1815. The 'Itinerary Rhine Tour' sketchbook (TB CLIX) contains a number of sketches used for details of the composition (fig.9c). Interestingly enough, the composition was already forecast in two minute leaves of the 'Itinerary Rhine Tour' sketchbook (fig.9b) and the 'Guards' sketchbook of 1817 (TB CLXIV 8), the

latter thus providing a tangible link with 'The Field of Waterloo'.

The scene as such, depicted from the lowest possible viewpoint, is realistic, with the packet-boat *The Swan* almost immobilised while waiting for the changing of the tide, and with villagers from the opposite shore offering fresh victuals to eager passengers, as was customary.

These two 'Dutch' oils may be seen to form a contrasted pair, the 'Field' symbolising Edmund Burke's 'Sublime' and the 'Dort', on the other hand, the 'Beautiful', or in Ruskin's terminology: 'Turner's two strengths in Terror and Repose'. Fellow Royal Academician Henry Thomson declared that the colours of the 'Dort' were so brilliant that it 'almost put your eyes out'. It was crucial in Turner's development, its high palette clearly being the bridgehead to the second half of his career.

Whether, as has been argued, it was really painted as a challenge to Augustus Wall Callcott's 'Entrance to the Pool of London' (fig.viii on p.18) is difficult to decide; that it was meant as a homage to Cuyp seems beyond doubt.

See also pp.17–18, above.

fig.9a Detail

fig.9b TB CLIX 50

fig.9c TB CLXII 77 verso

10 Entrance of the Meuse: Orange-Merchant on the Bar, Going to Pieces; Brill Church bearing S.E. by S., Masensluys E. by S., 1819*

Oil on canvas 175.3 × 246.4 (69 × 97)

Tate Gallery

N00501

B&J 139

fig.10a Detail

The title of this picture is remarkable for two reasons. First, there is the pun in the description of the wrecked merchant vessel: it is Dutch (the House of Orange), and holds a cargo of oranges. Then there is the topographical exactness of the painter's indication of the fatal sandbank. The co-ordinates given do indeed produce a fix on a danger spot in the Meuse estuary which can be seen marked by a wreck-buoy on contemporary charts (fig.10e). Also noteworthy is the focus of the picture itself, which is not the wreck but the scavenging fishermen.

The pun relates to the years 1818–19, when the British government's monetary manipulations of the Bank of England had included the end of gold circulation and the forced acceptance by the public of silver or banknotes. The Prince of Orange had invested heavily in England while exiled from Holland during the Napoleonic Wars. In the new economic set-up of the United Netherlands, King William I (formerly Prince William VI of Orange, and, because of his entrepreneurial acumen, soon referred to as the 'Merchant King'), wanted to convert his investments into cash for industrialisation. But the losses now incurred were a big and publicised disappointment, and frenzied salvage operations were launched to minimise the effect on the Dutch national economy. In his copy of Hills's *Sketches in Flanders and Holland*, Turner must have read about the author's own running aground, with a mention of the same two fishing ports here used in Turner's title, which he now used to lend authenticity to an imaginary event. The painting of the church of the Brill (fig.10a) and the sunny shoreline of 'Masensluys' (fig.10b) have been copied from his own impressions jotted down in 1817 in the 'Dort' sketchbook (fig.10c; the church on the horizon is Brill church). The elaborately rendered Cuypish cloud effects may be connected not only with further pages in the same sketchbook but also with his 'Skies' sketchbook of watercolour studies dating from 1818 and also the 'Haarlem from Spaarne' watercolour (fig.10d).

Turner's scavenging fishermen chasing floating oranges clearly embody another of his Dutch-inspired political quizzes. The idea may well have originated from a news item in the *Times* of 16 January 1819 which described the wreck off Whitehaven of a schooner carrying oranges. 'Entrance of the Meuse' is thus another illustration of the amazing combination of memory, association of thought, and urge to communicate topical feeling, which characterised so much of Turner's art.

See also pp.18–19, above.

fig.10b Detail

fig.10d 'Haarlem from Spaarne' (TB CCLXIII 197; D25319)

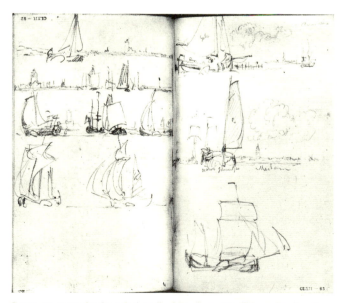

fig.10c TB CLXII 82, 83. p.83 inscribed (top image) 'yell' in mainsail and 'Maassluis' in sky; (middle image) 'de Vr[o]ue Jannetje' and 'Shedem' (Schiedem) along bottom

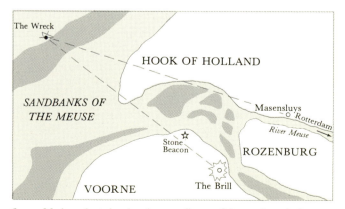

fig.10e Modern chart showing the co-ordinates of the wreck on the bar: Brill church bearing south-east by south, Masensluys east by south

11 **Port Ruysdael** exh.1827
Oil on canvas 92 × 122.5 (36¼ × 48¼)
Yale Center for British Art, Paul Mellon Collection
B&J 237

'Port Ruysdael' was universally admired, and Ruskin later declared: 'I know of no work at all comparable for the expression of the white, wild, cold, comfortless waves of the North Sea, even though the sea is almost subordinate to the awful rolling clouds' (*Modern Painters*, quoted B&J, p.237).

Like most Dutch painters of sea-coasts, Turner stuck to the formula of depicting in the foreground on the right a breakwater or pier-head as repoussoir, in this case with, on the left, the end to the other arm of a harbour entrance, marked by its starboard beacon – a motif directly reminiscent of Ruisdael's 'A Rough Sea', at the time in the Earl of Liverpool's collection. Like the majority of Ruisdael's seascapes, the impact in 'A Rough Sea' comes from the sharp contrast between light and dark. For Turner's strictures on composition as well as colour-scheme, see both his comment (p.19,

above) and his rapidly sketched and idiosyncratic copy of the Ruisdael in the Louvre (fig.11a), in the 'Studies in the Louvre' sketchbook, 1802 (fig.11b), with 'the house on the Embankment' omitted and 'the chief light … upon the surge in the foreground', as Turner noted, drastically reduced. Twenty-five years later criticism had turned into admiration. There is no place called Ruysdael; the artist's intention was evidently to express his homage to Ruisdael. In Turner's picture, there is no more than the slightest suggestion of a 'port', and this, together with the lee-shore under a threatening sky and the upset basket with spilled fish would seem to carry the usual message about the instability of physical existence in coastal Holland.

See also pp.19–20, above.

fig.11a Jacob van Ruisdael, 'Tempest on the Dutch Coast', 1660s
Musée du Louvre, Paris

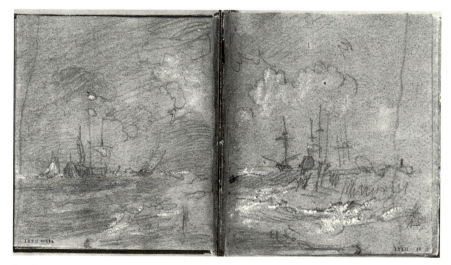

fig.11b TB LXXII 14 verso, 15

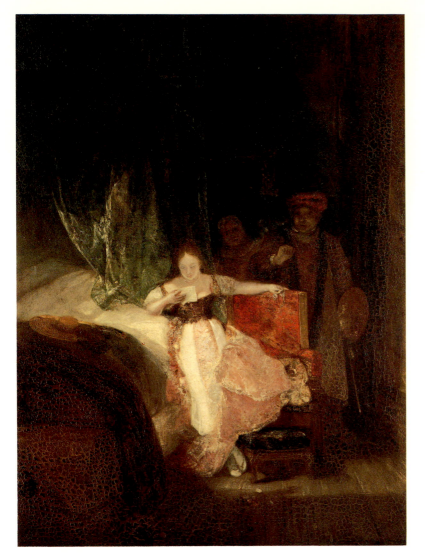

fig.12a Rembrandt van Rijn, 'Joseph and
Potiphar's Wife', 1655 *Gemäldegarlerie, Berlin*

12 Rembrandt's Daughter exh.1827
  Oil on canvas 122 × 86.3 (48 × 34)
  The Fogg Art Museum, Harvard University Art Museum,
  Gift of Edward W. Forbes
  B&J 238

Planned as an exercise in Rembrandtesque painting, this picture was based on Rembrandt's 'Joseph and Potiphar's Wife'
(fig.12a), owned at the time by Sir Thomas Lawrence. In its
style this is self-evident, but not in its content. The existence
of Rembrandt's daughter, Cornelia van Rijn, was not yet
known at this time, but the popularity of the Dutch painter
was such that all sorts of portraits were presented as Rembrandt relatives. The drama invented by Turner was the customary one of a father surprising his daughter reading a letter
from a suitor regarded as unworthy; what is curious is that
subsequently the secret facts of Rembrandt's life proved to
have been correctly guessed by Turner.

Except for the *Times*, the picture was ridiculed by the press.
However, it marked the revival of Turner's interest in Rem-
brandt, twenty years after he painted such genre pieces as
'The Unpaid Bill' (no.6) and 'The Garreteer's Petition' (Tate
Gallery; B&J 100).
  See also p.19, above.

13 Pilate Washing his Hands exh.1830*

Oil on canvas 91.5 × 121.9 (36 × 48)

Tate Gallery

N00510

B&J 332

In 1830 and 1832 Turner painted several biblical subjects, of which this is the finest and the most Rembrandtesque. The composition is unusual, and the components enigmatic: the crowd of figures does not appear to have any connection with the theme, and the title subject is placed high up in the background on the top left, stretching out his hands over a washbasin. The triumph of the picture is in its reinterpretation of Rembrandt's light, here given the leading role. The timescale is condensed: while Pilate makes his theatrical gesture, Christ is already staggering towards Golgotha. In the press it was called 'wretched and abortive', a joker declaring that 'a fine marine subject' would be a 'pilot washing his hands'.

14 Admiral Van Tromp's Barge at the Entrance of the Texel 1645 exh.1831

Oil on canvas 90.2 × 121.9 (25½ × 48)

Trustees of Sir John Soane's Museum, London

B&J 339

The first of a series of Dutch marine subjects, four of which represent 'Admiral Van Tromp', thereby confusing the father, Maarten Harpertsz[oon] Tromp (who was killed in action in 1653) with the son, Cornelis (who also became an Admiral). Their surname was simply 'Tromp', the 'Van' being a later addition, ensuing from their knighthoods. 'Sir Martin' was knighted by Charles I for escorting the Queen on her Dutch visit in 1642 to pawn the crown jewels, and the flamboyant son received a baronetcy from Charles II in recognition of his successes against the Barbary and Dunkirk pirates (see figs.x–xi on p.20).

The picture shows a state yacht entering the roadstead south of the island known as Texel, where convoys regularly assembled. In 1645 the accompanying squadron was under the command of the elder Tromp, who is shown about to board his flagship, prior to distinguishing himself again in protecting the Dutch merchant fleet and keeping the Dunkirk pirates in check.

The reason for Turner's renewed interest in Dutch marine history was most probably the 'betrayal' of the Dutch by the British Government at the outbreak of the Belgian Revolt in 1830. This led to a Dutch military operation in August, which aborted upon the threat of intervention by British and French forces. The result was the dissolution of the Kingdom of the United Netherlands, the final settlement only coming in December 1839. Turner's picture was evidently meant to recall a former successful alliance.

See also pp.20–1, above.

**15 Van Tromp's Shallop, at the Entrance
of the Scheldt** exh.1832
Oil on canvas 89 × 119.5 (35 × 47)
*Wadsworth Atheneum, Hartford, Connecticut. The Ella
Gallup Sumner and Mary Catlin Sumner Collection Fund*
B&J 344

A very curious composition, with the Admiral presumably
being rowed ashore, and an extraordinary flag flying in the
bows of the little boat. The ceremonial yacht in the centre has
an unusually curved bow, more English than Dutch. As a
painting, the picture is beautiful, however, and was generally
praised. The subject and composition once again show Turner's liking for painting Dutch-inspired historical marines that
also allowed him to make a political point.

See also pp.20–1, above.

16 Van Tromp Returning after the Battle off the Dogger Bank 1833*

Oil on canvas 90.5 × 120.6 (35⅝ × 47½)
Tate Gallery
N00537
B&J 351

The battle of the title is that of 6 July 1652, when the elder Tromp had been ordered to attack the English and Admiral Blake had successfully counter-attacked. This started the first Anglo–Dutch Sea War (1652–4). The picture shows a Dutch state barge (with anachronistic eighteenth-century rigging) lowering her jib while approaching Tromp's flagship, the Brederode. In the press the painting was praised for being 'clear, broad and chaste in colour and effect', the artist's wonted 'straw colour' having been replaced by a 'silvery tone'.

See also pp.20–1.

17 Van Tromp, Going about to Please his Masters, Ships a Sea, Getting a Good Wetting exh.1844
Oil on canvas 91.4 × 121.9 (36 × 48)
The J. Paul Getty Museum, Malibu, California
B&J 410

In 1666, Cornelis Tromp, son of Maarten Harpertz[oon] Tromp, was relieved of his command after failing to come to the aid of his superior, Admiral Michiel de Ruyter, having instead gone with his entire squadron in pursuit of more enemy warships. In 1673, William III, Supreme Commander of the Dutch forces in the war against Louis XIV and Charles I, succeeded in effecting a reconciliation: he persuaded Tromp to make his submission to the States General, offering to serve again in the interest of the country. In the picture this gesture is symbolised in the youthful Admiral 'going about', i.e. changing tack, in a heaving sea in which 'his masters' – the supreme government body of the Dutch Republic – remain unperturbed. Turner has used a good deal of imagination: flags with initials only came into fashion for merchant-captains in the nineteenth century, and an Admiral hanging on to a forestay, clad in white and waving his hat, would be too fanciful even for this maverick Tromp. The message of the picture is clearly that, in the hour of her need, a popular hero should swallow his wounded pride and again serve his country.

See also pp.22–3, above.

18 The Prince of Orange, William III, Embarked from Holland, and Landed at Torbay, November 4th, 1688 after a Stormy Passage exh.1832*

Oil on canvas 90.2 × 120 (35¹/₂ × 47¹/₄)

Tate Gallery. Presented by Robert Vernon 1847

N00369

B&J 343

Turner's rendering of this unique event in English history is impressive, but incorrect on a number of points. In October 1688, William's fleet had indeed been mauled by storms and had returned to base. On 1 November, however, he sailed in perfect weather, landing on 5 November without having fired a shot. In its review of the Royal Academy's 1832 exhibition, the *Examiner* referred not only to Turner's 'masterly sea-pieces', but also to his 'caricatures of history' – the nature of these caricatures remains undisclosed. There are certainly anachronisms, however. No Dutch long-boat would have had such a bow. The hat worn by the figure of William is of an eighteenth-century style (and in any case it would be impos-

sible to stand in such a heavy swell while raising one's hat in salute). Also, the boat is not flying his special standard: there is no suggestion of the specially adapted motto, 'Pro Religione et Libertate' – 'Je maintiendrai'.

Curiously, the critic of the *Athaneum* lamented on 26 May 1832 that 'the painter … has squandered his genius upon a subject which has lost somewhat of its feverish interest in the hearts of Englishmen'. The Dutch crisis was not the only association of thought expected to be called up by the picture. It was also a political allegory on the struggles of the Parliamentary Reform Bill 1832.

In the catalogue of the exhibition, Turner added to the title of his picture a reference to an unspecified 'History of England'. This probably referred to the five volume *History of England during the Reigns of King William, Queen Anne, and King George I 'by a Lover of Truth and Liberty'*, printed in 1744, which was in his friend Walter Fawkes's library at Farnley Hall. Another teaser is the incredible text, printed underneath the title and reading: 'The yacht in which His Majesty sailed was, after many changes and services, finally wrecked on Ham-

fig.18a Detail

burg sands, while employed in the Hull trade'. Turner must have believed that he was dealing with the royal yacht *Mary*, in which William had sailed home after his wedding to Mary on 4 November 1677 – which would account for the date in his title. And he must have confused this with the story of another former *Mary*, a royal yacht in which Princess Mary came over to join her husband for their coronation in 1689. Technically belonging to William, and sold under Queen Anne, she was turned into a freighter and renamed *Betsy Cains*. Wrecked off Teignmouth, the ship was finally broken up at Newcastle in 1827, an event which made the national press. On the strength of misleading articles in the *Newcastle Courant* of 24 February and 3 March, crowds of Williamite souvenir hunters appear to have been avidly buying up objects made from her timbers. Possibly Turner saw these articles and used them as the basis for his text. (See W. Senior, 'The Legend of the Betsy Cains', *Mariner's Mirror*, vol.1, no.1, 1911, pp.40–4 for an account of the story and a quotation from a verse cited in the paper: 'Behold the fate of sublunary things, / She exports coal that once imported Kings.')

Turner clearly wished his picture to appear as authentic as possible, creating this lengthy title with 'footnotes'. The legendary vicissitudes of the yacht *Mary* made a fascinating tale of fame and decline. It may not be too bold to assume that the feeling behind Turner's choice of quotation in the catalogue may possibly be an indication of what was one day to lead to 'The Fighting "Temeraire" Tugged to her Last Berth to be Broken Up, 1838' exh.1839 (National Gallery; B&J 377). His 'Prince of Orange' expresses triumph (the 'landing') over adversity ('after a stormy passage'), but the picture's sub-text is only seemingly optimistic; although politically Whiggish and therefore a supporter of the House of Orange, Turner was also the poet of *The Fallacies of Hope*. Perhaps, to him, even the most spectacular triumph was ultimately limited – in the added note the quotation suggests that, in spite of his applauding the success of a bold undertaking, Turner knows that at its core this success must inevitably harbour the seeds of transience, decay and death.

See also p.21, above.

**19 Helvoetsluys; – the City of Utrecht, 64,
Going to Sea** exh.1832
Oil on canvas 91.4 × 122 (36 × 48)
Private Collection
B&J 345

The sixty-four-gun warship City of Utrecht was the flagship of one of the Prince of Orange's Lt.-Admirals in 1688. The port of Hellevoetsluis was the principal naval base and even in Turner's time a popular terminal for ferry services to Britain; in 1817 Turner copied a few references to Hellevoetsluis in his 'Itinerary Rhine Tour' sketchbook (TB CLIX). In the painting the town, which should appear on the right, is not visible, but on the left the tower of the island of Goeree, across from the harbour and sketched in the 'Holland' sketchbook (TB CCXIV), is correctly depicted. There is an anecdote about how Turner, on the Royal Academy's Varnishing Day, saw Constable's colourful 'Opening of Waterloo Bridge' (Tate Gallery), which was hung next to his work. He

quickly added a blob of red lead on his grey sea, shaping it to look like a bouy, and left. Constable is reported to have said: 'He has been here, and fired a gun.'

The choice of subject was clearly meant to reinforce the artist's intentions behind 'Van Tromp's Shallop' (no.15) and 'The Prince of Orange' (no.18), i.e. to remind his compatriots of a time when they had markedly benefited from a Dutch initiative.

See also p.21, above.

20 The Rotterdam Ferry Boat exh.1833
Oil on canvas 92.7 × 123.2 (36½ × 48½)
Ailsa Mellon Bruce Collection.
National Gallery of Art, Washington
B&J 348

This curious composition shows a little sailboat transporting women and children, and also a seventeenth-century man-of-war at anchor, bristling with guns run out. In the distant background is the Rotterdam waterfront (figs.20a–b), dominated by the tower of the church of St Lawrence. What is remarkable is the little boat which appears 'manned' only by women and children. The composition seems to suggest the safe passage from shore to shore of even the physically weaker members of the community in a centre of hard-bitten commerce, backed by the arms of tradition.

See also p.22, above.

fig.20a Detail

fig.20b TB CLXII 14a, 15

**21 [Antwerp;] Van Goyen Looking out for
a Subject** exh.1833
Oil on canvas 91.8 × 122.9 (36⅛ × 48⅜)
The Frick Collection, New York
B&J 350

Turner had travelled through Antwerp in 1817 in order to
enter the Northern Netherlands by the Rotterdam mail-
coach, as indicated by the sketches in his 'Dort' sketchbook
(TB CLXII; figs.21a–b). Although 'Antwerp' was not part of the
original title, this painting is unmistakably a view of the
Antwerp waterfront from the river Scheldt. The Dutch Master Van Goyen did indeed visit the city (which before Rotterdam was the chief commercial port of the Southern
Netherlands) and was no doubt looking for a subject to paint.
But he would not have worn a richly plumed hat on board,
and it is also implausible that any seventeenth-century vessel
would have 'Van G' painted on its stern (which Turner uses
as a device to identify the subject beyond doubt), or have such
heavy double rubbing strakes.

The message would have been about Dutch creative artists
still being free to select their themes, even in a Belgian mer-
cantile concentration of long-standing and complicated by
political conflicts.

Whether this work was painted before or after the 'Rotterdam Ferry Boat' (no.20) is unclear, but with the similarity in
their composition and typical ambiance and function of the
cities in the two countries a close connection seems undeni-
able. Both pictures were very favourably received.

See also p.22, above.

fig.21a TB CLXII 2a–3

fig.21b TB CLXII 5a–6

**22 Fishing Boats Bringing a Disabled Ship into
Port Ruysdael** exh.1844*

Oil on canvas 91.4 × 123.2 (36 × 48½)

Tate Gallery

N00536

B&J 408

In 1827 Turner had painted 'Port Ruysdael' (no.11). Even earlier, in 1802, he had filled four pages of his 'Studies in the Louvre' sketchbook with written and sketched memoranda of
two pictures by Ruisdael, a seascape and a landscape (see
above pp.19–20, and fig.11b on p.47), at the exhibition of
Napoleon's stolen art treasures from his European cam-
paigns. When in 1827 the spirit moved Turner to compose a
picture in homage to this revered Dutch artist, the words 'Sea
[gap] Port [gap] Rysdale', which he had inscribed in the
'Studies in the Louvre' sketchbook, may have given him the
idea, while its composition owes much to Ruisdael's characteristic seapieces.

In this painting, the small fishing boats are racing to the
big, apparently 'disabled', ship lying hove-to in the background. The crews are keen on salvage money, knowing that
a safe haven is within easy reach, indicated by the beacon on
the right.

In a letter to his agent, Turner referred to this picture as
'the new Port Ruysdael', enquiring whether it 'shall be with
fish only, and if the new Marine Pictures are to have Dutch
Boats only' (Turner to Thomas Griffith, 1 February 1844).

See also p.23, above.

23 Ostend exh.1844

Oil on canvas 92.9 × 123.2 (36½ × 48½)

Bayerische Staatsgemäldesammlungen,
Neue Pinakothek, Munich

B&J 407

Painted in Turner's favourite atmospheric style, this picture presents a final example of 'Sublimity' in a one-time (until 1839) Dutch context. The little sailboat in the centre seems about to be smashed against the western arm of Ostend's outer harbour. Only a last-minute gibe of her mainsail will enable the helmsman to 'claw off' and to follow the others into port; it is this manouevre that is Turner's subject. In 1844, on his last trip to Switzerland, the artist jotted down a few quick sketches of Ostend in his 'Ostend, Rhine and Wurzburg' and 'Ostend, Rhine and Berne' sketchbooks (TB CCCIII, TB CCCXXVII; figs.23a, 23b). The *Spectator* rightly praised Turner for 'the daring originality of his effects'.

Together with 'Fishing Boats Bringing a Disabled Ship into Port Ruysdael' (no.22), his 'Ostend' is the last direct expression of Turner's Dutch allegiance: with his depiction of the port through which in 1817 he first entered the Netherlands he seems to have come full circle, and at the same time returning to his home-port in the knowledge that he had absorbed fully what Dutch art had to offer – no matter how much or how little 'disabled' by age.

See also p.23, above.

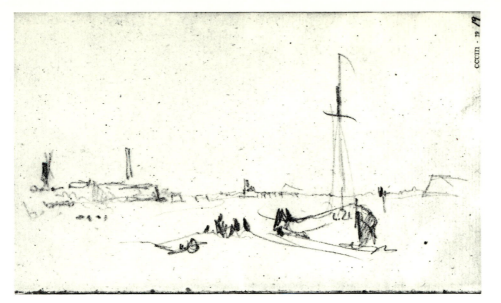

fig.23a TB CCCIII 19

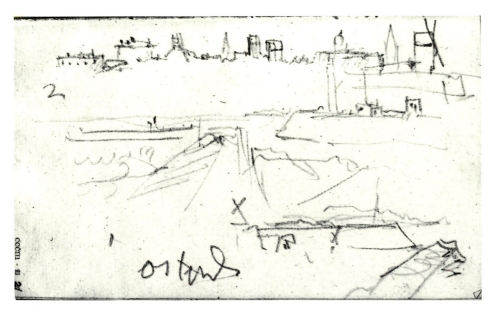

fig.23b TB CCCIII 21

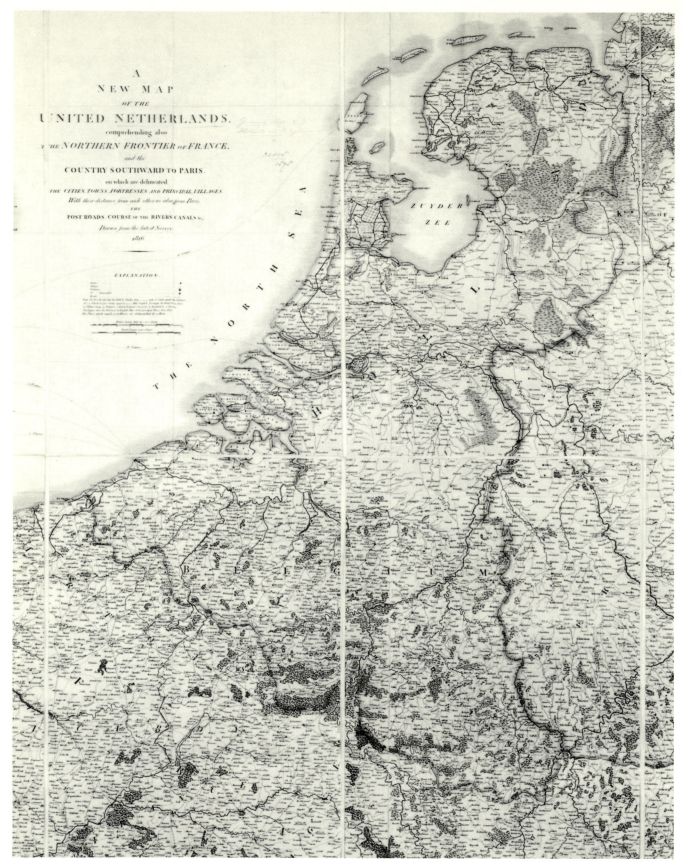

'A New Map of the United Netherlands' 1816
The British Library Board

Selected Topographical Sketches

Scheveningen beach with fishing-folk
('Dort' sketchbook, TB CLXII 27)

Ghent, church of St Michael
('Waterloo and Rhine' sketchbook, TB CLX 3 verso, 4)

Haarlem, Amsterdam Gate
('Dort' sketchbook, TB CLXII 41 verso)

Amsterdam, memorandum of Terborch's
'Parental Visit' ('Holland' sketchbook, TB CCXIV 81)

Four views from east of Dordrecht. Inscribed 'Cuyp'
('Holland' sketchbook, TB CCXIV 60 verso)

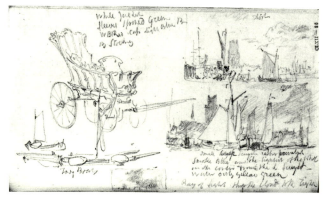

Amsterdam, Royal Palace. Inscribed 'Storks' [kept to clean fishmarket]
('Holland' sketchbook, TB CCXIV 98 verso)

Dordrecht, farmer's cart and three sketches of 'Dort'.
Inscribed 'Ray of Light through Cloud on the right [etc.]'
('Dort' sketchbook, TB CLXII 86)

Amsterdam, Realen Eiland off river Y
('Holland' sketchbbook, TB CCXIV 103 verso)

Amsterdam, Schreiers Toren
('Holland' sketchbook, TB CCXIV 105)

Rotterdam, church of St Lawrence
('Dort' sketchbook, TB CLXII 17 verso, 18)

Rotterdam, Delftsevaart ('Rotterdam'
sketchbook, TB CCCXXI 4 verso)

Rotterdam, Laurensstraat ('Rotterdam'
sketchbook, TB CCCXXI 20 verso)

Market wares
('Dort' sketchbook, TB CLXII 60)

Coastal profiles
('Holland' sketchbook, TB CCXIV 29 verso)

Shipping on the Meuse off Rotterdam
('Holland' sketchbook, TB CCXIV 45 verso)

Studies of Dutch womenfolk
('Holland' sketchbook, TB CCXIV 65)

List of Exhibited Works

All works are by J.M.W. Turner unless otherwise stated. Dimensions are given in centimetres followed by inches in brackets; height before width. Measurements for the sketchbooks are given as closed sizes.

'Calais Pier, with French Poissards Preparing for Sea; An English Packet Arriving' exh.1803
Oil on canvas 172 × 240 (64¾ × 94½)
Trustees of the National Gallery, London
[no.2, p.30]

'Sun Rising through Vapour; Fishermen Cleaning and Selling Fish' exh.1807
Oil on canvas 134.5 × 179 (53 × 70½)
Trustees of the National Gallery, London
[no.5, p.34]

'The Field of Waterloo' exh.1818
Oil on canvas 147.5 × 238.8 (58 × 94)
Tate Gallery
N00500
[no.7, p.37]

'The Field of Waterloo "Hougoumont"' 1819
Watercolour on paper 28.7 × 38.8 (11¼ × 15¼)
Syndics of the Fitzwilliam Museum, Cambridge
[no.8, p.40]

'Entrance of the Meuse: Orange-Merchant on the Bar, Going to Pieces; Brill Church bearing S.E. by S., Masensluys E. by S.' 1819
Oil on canvas 175.3 × 246.4 (69 × 97)
Tate Gallery
N00501
[no.10, p.44]

'Pilate Washing his Hands' exh.1830
Oil on canvas 91.4 × 121.9 (36 × 48)
Tate Gallery
N00510
[no.13, p.49]

'Van Tromp Returning after the Battle off the Dogger Bank' 1833
Oil on canvas 90.5 × 120.6 (35⅝ × 47½)
Tate Gallery
N00537
[no.16, p.52]

'The Prince of Orange, William III, Embarked from Holland, and Landed at Torbay, November 4th, 1688 after a Stormy Passage' exh.1832
Oil on canvas 90.2 × 120 (35½ × 47¼)
Tate Gallery. Presented by Robert Vernon 1847
N00369
[no.18, p.54]

'Fishing Boats Bringing a Disabled Ship into Port Ruysdael' exh.1844
Oil on canvas 91.4 × 123.2 (36 × 48½)
Tate Gallery
N00536
[no.22, p.61]

After Willem Van de Velde
'A Kaag Going to Windward in a Fresh Breeze'
Oil on canvas 67.5 × 112 (26½ × 44)
National Maritime Museum, Greenwich

'Fishermen at Sea' exh.1796
Oil on canvas 91.4 × 122.2 (36 × 48⅛)
Tate Gallery. Purchased 1972
T01585
[ex cat.]

'The Garreteer's Petition' exh.1809
Oil on panel 55.2 × 79.1 (21¾ × 31⅛)
Tate Gallery
N00482
[ex cat.]

Works on Paper

'Entrance of Calais Harbour' 1816
from Etchings and Engravings for the *Liber Studiorum*
Mezzotint: image size 17.9 × 26.7 (7 × 10½)
Tate Gallery. Presented by A. Acland Allen through the National
Art Collections Fund 1925
A01116
[no.3a, p.32]

William Miller after J.M.W. Turner
'Hougoumont'
from Scott's *Miscellaneous Prose* 1834–6, vol.v
Engraving 10 × 8.8 (4 × 3½)
Dr Jan Piggott
[no.8a, p.41]

Edward Finden after J.M.W. Turner
'The Field of Waterloo. From Hougoumont' pub.1833
Engraving
Tate Gallery. Transferred from the British Museum 1988
T06185
[no.8b, p.41]

'Haarlem from Spaarne'
Gouache on paper 18.5 × 22.9 (7¼ × 9)
Tate Gallery
TB CCLXII 197
D25319
[no.10d, p.45]

Elisha Kirkall after Willem Van de Velde
'Gust of Wind'
Mezzotint: plate size 43.1 × 31.2 (17 × 12¼)
National Maritime Museum, Greenwich
[fig.i, p.12]

J. Houbraken after Jan Lievens
'Maarten Harpertszoon Tromp'
Engraving 22 × 15 (8⅝ × 5⅞)
Private Collection
[fig.x, p.20]

J. Houbraken after Jan Lievens
'Kornelis Tromp'
Engraving 22 × 15 (8⅝ × 5⅞)
Private Collection
[fig.xi, p.20]

Charles Campbell
The Traveller's Complete Guide through Belgium and Holland 1817
The British Library Board

Sketchbooks from the Turner Bequest

'Calais Pier' (TB LXXXI)
43.3 × 27.2 (17 × 10¾)
D04902–05072

'Studies in the Louvre' (TB LXXII)
12.9 × 6.4 (5⅛ × 2½)
D04275–04390

'Waterloo and Rhine' (TB CLX)
15 × 9.5 (5⅞ × 3¾)
D12702–12883

'Itinerary Rhine Tour' (TB CLIX)
5.6 × 10.5 (2¼ × 4⅛)
D12528–12701

'Dort' (TB CLXII)
15.6 × 9.3 (6¼ × 3⅝)
D12996–13170

'Guards' (TB CLXIV)
6.9 × 10.3 (2⅜ × 4)
D13245–13321

'Holland' (TB CCXIV)
15.5 × 9.5 (6⅛ × 3¾)
D18841–19400

'Rotterdam' (TB CCCXXI)
15.3 × 9.5 (6 × 3¾)
D32444–32540

'Rotterdam and Rhine' (TB CCCXXI)
17 × 10.5 (6⅝ × 4⅛)
D32541–32663

Lenders

British Library
Fitzwilliam Museum, Cambridge
National Gallery, London
National Maritime Museum, Greenwich
Jan Piggott
Tate Gallery

Photographic Credits

Jorg P. Anders
Algemeen Rijksarchief, The Hague
Fred Bachrach
Bayerische Staatsgemäldesammlungen, Munich
Staatliche Museen zu Berlin – Preußischer Kulturbesitz
British Library Reproductions
The Corcoran Gallery of Art, Washington
Fitzwilliam Museum, Cambridge
The Fogg Art Museum, Harvard University
The Frick Collection, New York
The J. Paul Getty Museum, Malibu
The Paul Mellon Center for Studies in British Art
National Maritime Museum, Greenwich
National Gallery, London
National Portrait Gallery, London
Agence Photographique de la Réunion des Musées
    Nationaux, Paris
Rijksmuseum-Stichting, Amsterdam
Patricia Schindler
Graham Snape
Sir John Soane's Museum, London
Tate Gallery Photographic Department
Toledo Museum of Art
Wadsworth Atheneum, Hartford
National Gallery of Art, Washington
V & A Picture Library
Victoria University of Manchester, Tabley House
Yale Center for British Art